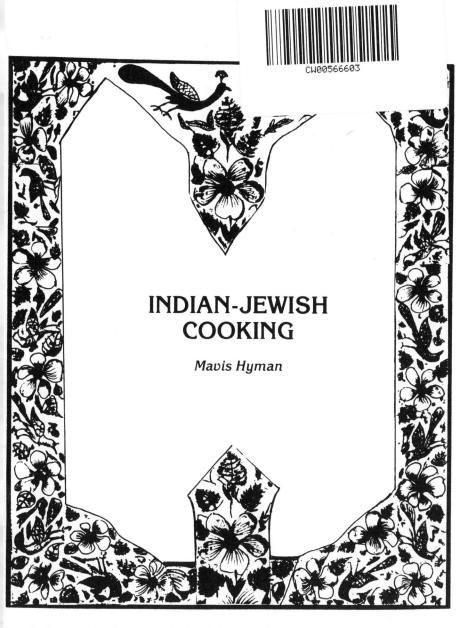

INDIAN-JEWISH COOKING

Mavis Hyman

Border reproduced from part of the 'kettubah' — marriage certificate (1897) of Meir Ezra and Masooda Musleah, grand-parents of the author.

The front cover photograph is by John Hyman.

It shows typical dishes for Friday nights or Festivals. Benedictions over wine and bread precede the meal. The "tiryah" or seven oil lamps, lit on the eve of these occasions is suspended from the ceiling. The "tiryah" is by courtesy of Mr and Mrs David Einy. The bread cover was embroidered for the author by her aunt, Ramah Musleah, to celebrate New Year.

Illustrations by Mavis Hyman.
© Mavis Hyman.

First published in August 1992.
Reprinted in October 1992, May 1993, August 2000

Printed by The Guernsey Press Co. Ltd., Guernsey, C.I.

Hyman Publishers
10 Holyoake Walk
London N2 0JX

ISBN 0 9518150 0 8

BIOGRAPHICAL NOTE

Mavis Hyman was born in Calcutta and both her parents were of Iraqi-Jewish origin. She is directly descended on her mother's side from one of the earliest Jewish settlers in Calcutta some 200 years ago. She emigrated to the United Kingdom in 1957, is married and has two daughters.

She graduated from the London School of Economics in 1966 and was later awarded a Masters degree from there. She has worked in colleges in London University as a sociologist, researching in areas of social care.

Mrs Hyman paints in oils, has exhibited her work and has had a one-woman show. She is self-taught in painting, specialises in impressionistic and stylised landscape, and recently in Indian themes.

The impetus for this cookery book came more from a desire to preserve this part of her tradition than from a particular expertise in cooking as such. The history, liturgy and mourning traditions of this community over its 200 year period of existence have been documented by Mrs Hyman's cousin, Rabbi Ezekiel Musleah. This work on cooking contributes towards the preservation of customs in this fragment of Jewry.

The unmistakeable pleasure which guests from outside the community have continued to show at her table for more than thirty years, lead her to believe that the style of cooking on which she was raised should be shared with as many people as possible.

In loving memory of my mother, Mozelle,
and
for my daughters, Esther and Miriam.

Contents

Introduction

Brick and clay fire

Introduction

There has been an explosion in publications on cooking since the late 1950s so that both regional and international cuisine are well explored. Yet the demand remains unabated and the boundaries continue to be extended. Most of the recipes here are being widely published for the first time in this country and they stem from my experience of coming from a relatively small and perhaps little known Jewish community. The experience is fairly typical of Jews in the diaspora and is the story of migration from one country to another, some movements being followed by fairly long periods of stability. My family went to India from Baghdad and this history is documented by my cousin, Rabbi Ezekiel N Musleah in "On the Banks of the Ganga : Sojourn of Jews in Calcutta". I am indebted to him for the historical background to this work.

For centuries Baghdad was the foremost centre in the Middle East for Jewish learning and cultural development, and this was possible largely because Jews enjoyed stable settlement in that part of the world from the time of the destruction of the First Temple until very recent years. This community, which had a uniquely uninterrupted life for 2500 years approximately, is now largely dispersed. What we know today as Iraq and Syria had been a trading area with India for centuries. Spices and indigo from South East Asia, including the Indian sub-continent, attracted rich business dealings. In addition, the numerous Indian princes and their families provided a constant and lucrative market for precious stones and jewellery. These trading opportunities were the main incentive for Jewish settlement in India from the Middle East. My own family were among the group of traders who left Baghdad to settle in Calcutta. Like other minority groups in India, the Jewish community of Iraqi and Syrian origins maintained its own identity while living peaceably with Hindus, Muslims and people of many other faiths for 200 years.

The three main centres of Jewish settlement in India were Bombay, Cochin and Calcutta. Those in Bombay and in Cochin, both on the Western coast, were of ancient origin and their early histories are speculative and bound up with legend. Documentation in the last few hundred years informs us of more recent history and development and in both Bombay and Cochin there were different groups of Jewish settlement with diverse backgrounds. In Bombay the Bene Israel (Children of Israel) were distinct from the Jews of Iraqi origin and each community had their own traditions with largely separate social lives. Although the Iraqi Jews were far fewer in number than the Bene Israel they exerted considerable influence and were concerned with the expansion of religious education. There is documentary evidence of Jewish settlement in Cranganore, twenty miles north of Cochin in "a set of copper plates (which still exist) whose date is variously indicated as 379 C.E. and 750 C.E. This twenty-seven square mile territory was perhaps the only sovereign Jewish principality in almost two thousand years of diaspora. The Jews became well established and very influential. They made many converts from among the natives and generally from their slaves."[1] Even from very early days there was a division amongst the Jewish community — a division between masters and slaves. The separation between the white and black Cochin Jews persisted through the ages until the present time.

Cochin was the centre of the spice trade and as such was particularly prized in the period of European colonisation. There were settlers from Spain and Portugal, from Holland and Britain, and last but not least from Iraq. Among the settlers were white Jews and as their history suggests, their background was chequered. However, the fact that the Iraqis were in the last wave of settlement has meant that their customs and traditions came to be largely dominant in Cochin. By contrast, Jewish settlement in Calcutta by Jews from Syria and Iraq in the main, dated from the eighteenth century and this history is well documented. Generally speaking, the traditions and customs of Iraq assumed importance in the Jewish communities in India, located principally in Bombay, Cochin and Calcutta.

So far as cuisine was concerned, the food of the Bene Israel was said to be virtually indistinguishable from that of the native population. The Jews in Bombay and in Cochin who had come from Iraq, and the Jews in Calcutta, shared the same cultural heritage and any differences in cuisine were ones of detail rather than fundamental. The Jews in Bombay and Cochin had facilities for the slaughter of large animals which were lacking in Calcutta and as such they were able to retain the meat dishes in their repertoire which were enjoyed in Baghdad. In spite of the fact that the Jews of Cochin had a mixed history of settlement, their cuisine came to be largely influenced by Iraqis. The differences in their food arise mainly from their geographic location. Like other South Indians, they like their food very chillie-hot, they cook mainly in coconut oil and use coconut and coconut milk in many dishes. Fresh fish was plentiful as in other coastal towns, and a wider range of fish dishes could be found in Cochin, as in Bombay, than in the community in Calcutta. The names of many dishes from Cochin are similar to those used in the Iraqi communities in Bombay and Calcutta, but some have Malayalam names — the language of South India, and these will be indicated in the relevant sections here. During the nineteenth century the black Jews in Cochin rebelled more than once against the white Jews "challenging the authority of the whites to discriminate"[2] against them. Many left Cochin for Bombay and Calcutta where they were employed as domestic servants by the Jewish communities. The quality of life was much more acceptable to the black Cochin Jews in their new surroundings as the Iraqi Jews did not have the experience or tradition of owning slaves. These Jews from Cochin became excellent cooks and were taught by women who had come from Baghdad. This was one way in which the black Jews of Cochin became expert in, and carriers of, traditional Iraqi cooking.

Until the early twentieth century the majority of Jews of Iraqi origin and the white Jews of Cochin were engaged in commercial activities, but gradually more people became attracted to the professions. After the Second World War there were fundamental political and social changes in India. Independence from Britain and the partition of the country created considerable unrest in the late 1940s. At that time there were few impediments to migration and many young Jews decided to go abroad to work or to obtain professional qualifications. England — which had until then been the "mother country" was often the first choice. After becoming qualified, most of the young people found employment in the West and they had grown accustomed and attracted to their new way of life. As they became reluctant to return to their relatively small communities in India their parents began to join them instead. At the same time the state of Israel was established and Jews were welcomed there from all parts of the world.

Air lifts were arranged by the Jewish Agency and in many cases entire families departed to Israel, convinced that the future for them lay there. Others were attracted to a new life in Australia and a few found opportunities to work and live in the United States. It should be emphasised that those who left were not forced to do so but were attracted to what they thought were wider opportunities abroad. Those who return now do so as travellers with many happy memories.

Characteristically, Jewish communities in the diaspora preserved their culture with interesting culinary results. In the Middle East, for example, Jews had a repertoire of dishes indigenous to that region and which they took with them to lands of new settlement. From the time they left Baghdad and Syria until the present day, most of the Jews in India retain an essentially Middle Eastern style of cooking. The connections are clear, from the works of Elizabeth David[3], Claudia Roden[4], Susie Benghiat[5], and Daisy Iny[6] for example. During the 200 years of settlement, however, Indian influences inevitably crept in. The employment of Moslem cooks in Jewish households meant not only that the cooks learnt our way of cooking but they also introduced to us local dishes, local ingredients, and local traditions in cooking. Since Hindus are generally vegetarian, their dishes are compatible with "kashrut" or ritually permissible foods for Jews. Some Indian foods therefore became wholly adopted in our own repertoire, such as the range of bread for example — chapatees, purees, paratas, etc. Recipes for these foods will be found in books specifically on Indian cookery. Where recipes have been modified, a hybrid cooking has emerged and these will be included here. The mainspring of this work, however, lies in the style of cooking brought from Baghdad and Syria to the three main Jewish settlements in India — Bombay, Cochin and Calcutta.

In my own lifetime there has been a gradual but almost complete disintegration of the Jewish community in Calcutta. The situation has been much the same for the white Jewish community in Cochin and the black Jews also emigrated in large numbers to Israel. "The Cochin Jews were imbued with the spirit of Zionism. (This) made them uproot themselves from a self-supporting environment ... (and) in transmitting their communal assets to Israel they became one of the most provided for groups of immigrants."[7] Like the Cochin Jews, the Bene Israel community were also inspired by Zionism. "... in two decades ... their population in India had been reduced by half".[8] Large numbers of Bombay Jews of Iraqi origin also emigrated to Israel, England and other Western countries but a nucleus still remains.

Like many other immigrants, people from the Iraqi-Indian communities brought their own style of cooking to the places of new settlement in the West. This is quite distinctive and is little known in this part of the world. Yet even in the three decades in which I have lived in this country the form of cooking on which I was reared is gradually changing its character, not only because of differences in the variety of ingredients, changes in cooking apparatus, and a greater awareness and appreciation of European cooking, but also because competing demands limit the time spent on cooking. In Calcutta, cooks in any household had a full time job and they were sometimes assisted by an under cook and the mistress of the house. The changes we have experienced in this country have affected cooking methods in particular so that even though traditional cooking may be preferred to others, short cuts are rapidly being introduced. In most homes in Calcutta the cooking was done on brick and clay fires so that oven cooking was difficult to achieve and even more difficult to control. It did not take us long to appreciate and exploit oven cooking when we came to this country. Whether or not the quality of our cooking is being affected by the changes we are making is a moot point.

Clearly cooking styles change and develop for lesser reasons than migration. Even within a small community there are many variations in cooking particular dishes from one family to another. One of the great attractions of cooking is that it is enriched by these variations. This collection of recipes is therefore essentially personal and to emphasise the point I show variations as I have learnt them from others. I hope this will encourage readers to use these recipes flexibly — more as a guide to the style it represents rather than as a prescriptive approach to preparing food.

The intention is to preserve in essence, a form of cookery which has been bound up with a particular ethnic group for many generations. This is not difficult to justify. These recipes are for dishes which are enjoyed not only by those reared on them but also by those who are complete strangers to them. The sheer enjoyment of eating is spread, not in the sense of a haute cuisine but in the everyday domestic scene. While we lived in relatively large numbers in India our cooking traditions were passed on from generation to generation — if not from mother to daugher, then from father to son among the community of cooks who worked in our homes. The almost complete dispersion of the Jewish community in Iraq, and even its off-shoots in India means that the very sources of our style of cooking are scarcely in existence any longer. Although my cooking is rooted in my own tradition, it is no longer exclusively so. As my children become exposed to increasingly different influences they too will adopt a style of cooking which becomes even further removed from its source. If these recipes are not written down now they will not be preserved and will become forgotten sooner or later.

The observance of Jewish dietary laws means that certain foods are excluded, such as shell fish and cuts of meat from a pig. Meat and milk produce are not cooked together. We have compensated for this exclusiveness by learning to be more imaginative with what we can use and this could open up interesting avenues for more people. Vegetarians, for example, will find a new range of dishes. Now that vegetables, fruit, and even frozen fish from warmer countries are readily available here, many Europeans will wish to know of different ways in which they may be prepared. Produce such as lady's fingers (bindie or bamia), aubergine (kala began), fresh coriander leaves (dhunnia putta), etc are now a familiar part of the greengrocery scene in many districts of large and small towns in this country. Facilities for the ritual slaughter of larger animals were very limited in Calcutta and so we had to become more inventive in cooking poultry and fish. This could be of use to those who want to cut down on red meat and who look to alternative sources of protein which are at least more economical. It is not just our style of cooking which is different — our eating styles are different too. Our meals did not consist of three or four courses served in a set order. Instead a variety of freshly cooked dishes was placed on the dining-table and passed round, both at lunch and at dinner. Fresh fruit generally came at the end of the meal. But the Western reader need not be dismayed for these recipes can fit in quite comfortably with eating patterns in this part of the world. There are a variety of foods which will make acceptable starters or entree dishes and which are included in the section on "Light Meals". Vegetable and other stews and soups can be served as a first course, particularly on cold days. Recipes in the section on "Main Meals" are suitable for the main course and in each section there are a number of vegetarian dishes. The savoury appetisers in the section on "Relishes" may be enjoyed equally with light or substantial meals. Although desserts, in the sense of 'afters' are not part of our tradition, sweet foods certainly are; these were often served as tea-time treats or as delicacies with coffee at any time friends happend to call. These recipes will be found under the section on "Sweets". Although domestic ovens were rare in Calcutta there were several highly skilled confectioners in the community who provided traditional specialities. The best known is Nahoum & Sons, still flourishing in the New Market in Calcutta by providing for all communities. There was also the itinerent baker, well tutored by the women who came from Baghdad, who prepared the goodies at home and then carried them off to his bakery to cook.

There are foods which have become associated with particular occasions, to mark personal celebrations and religious holidays, such as baklawa for weddings, aloo makalla, hushwa, roast chicken, mahasha, and halba for the eve of sabbath, humeen cooked overnight on a very low flame to provide a hot meal for the sabbath day. A separate section on "Foods for Festivals" sets the food in a socio-religious context. These recipes are worth having in their own right and also make interesting comparison with Jewish communities of different origins and experience.

Ethnic groups coming to Britain have brought with them a wealth of their own culture, expressed in music, art, drama, cookery, etc. One of the earliest of these groups was the Jews. Yet even European Jews who have been living here for many generations are not widely aware of the existence in this country of ancient communities of the Middle East and Asia with entirely different styles of cooking. Their cultural heritage is distinct in many ways, not least in their food.

The dishes brought to you here will enable you to share in, and even preserve part of a very old culinary tradition. In doing so you will be able to enjoy a style of cooking which may be new and unfamiliar but hopefully, well worth knowing.

References :

1. Musleah, Rabbi E.N. (1975). "On the Banks of the Ganga: The Sojourn of Jews in Calcutta". The Christopher Publishing House, Massachusetts. p. 359.
2. Op. cit. p.369.

3. David, Elizabeth. (1988 Revised) "A Book of Mediterranean Food". Dorling Kindersley.
4. Roden, C. (1985) "A New Book of Middle Eastern Food". Penguin.
5. Benghiat, S. (1984) "Middle Eastern Cookery". Weidenfeld.
6. Iny, D. (1976) "The Best of Baghdad Cooking". E P Dutton & Co Inc.
7. Musleah, E.N. Op. cit. p. 375.
8. Musleah, E.N. Op.cit. p. 389.

Preparing spices the traditional way

"Tawa" - heavy pan for roasting spice seeds

"Seal" - grinding stones for herbs, spices and pulses

"Hamam dusta" - pestle and mortar, made in brass, for pounding spices

Acknowledgements

The recipes here have been collected and assembled over a period of two years. I started with the intention of doing this for my daughters but as I discussed the project with friends and relatives I was encouraged to believe there would be wider interest. I therefore set out to record not only those dishes with which I was personally familiar but to cover as wide a range as I could identify within the community of Indian Jews in Bombay, Calcutta and Cochin. This was achieved by consulting many people, particularly those of my mother's generation. There have been some difficulties in finding people with the know-how in preparing certain dishes, and then getting them right, but overall there has been immense enjoyment and satisfaction. This is largely because of the enthusiasm of so many people who readily became involved. There were cooking sessions with friends to try out and record the recipes, introductions to people with particular expertise, recipes and advice received from far and wide, and many opportunities for tasting dishes which were new to me.

Unfortunately, some of the people who helped me so generously are no longer alive. Most of the friends who worked with me to test the recipes wish to remain anonymous. It would be difficult to single out only a few individuals and thank them by name since I enjoyed advice and assistance from numerous people. It seems more appropriate, therefore, to acknowledge my gratitude and appreciation in a general way to the experts, and to friends and family for their enthusiastic support.

OVEN TEMPERATURE EQUIVALENTS

Fahrenheit (degrees)	Centigrade (degrees)	Gas	Heat
225	110	$\frac{1}{4}$	Very cool
250	130	$\frac{1}{2}$	Very cool
275	140	1	Cool
300	150	2	Cool
325	160	3	Moderate
350	180	4	Moderate
375	190	5	Fairly hot
400	200	6	Fairly hot
425	220	7	Very hot
450	230	8	Very hot

EQUIVALENTS OF SOLID INGREDIENTS

Flour	1 cup	=	5 - 6 ozs.	=	150 - 175 grams
White sugar	1 cup	=	8 ozs.	=	250 grams
Brown sugar	1 cup	=	6 ozs.	=	175 grams
Butter/margarine	1 cup	=	8 ozs.	=	250 grams
Rice	1 cup	=	7 ozs.	=	200 grams

Relishes

The traditional way of preparing pickles

Large amounts of vegetables, herbs and spices

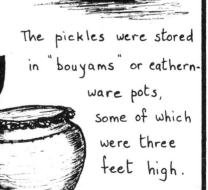

cooked in large "karais" on small bucket fires. Metal buckets, lined with clay and coal fired.

The pickles were stored in "bouyams" or eathernware pots, some of which were three feet high.

RELISHES whet the appetite and the range here includes typical Middle Eastern sauces, chillie hot for those who prefer them that way; vegetables pickled in brine or vinegar with chillies, garlic, ginger and other herbs, and the hot spiced varieties in an oil base which have a distinct Indian influence.

Many main and light dishes are neither spiced nor chillie-hot and the addition of relishes provides this extra for those who enjoy them. However, it is perfectly possible to make relishes without adding chillies. It is not uncommon to eat some sauces with bread alone, since they become infused with the aroma of the spices and the vegetables, or to nibble on pickles as one would on nuts or crisps.

Although some of these relishes will appear to be familiar, for example the vegetables pickled in brine or vinegar, the particular herbs and spice mixtures suggested here make the flavours unique. The vegetables or mix of vegetables used in these recipes of spiced pickles are unlikely to be found on the shelves of grocery stores and those which are commercially produced are made to different recipes. The spiced pickles are easy and quick to make at home, most people prefer them, and they come much cheaper this way.

Coriander Leaf Chutney
(Dhunia Chutney)

Wash and pick over *6 ozs of fresh coriander leaves and stems.* Chop coarsely. Cover the blades of a liquidiser with *cold water,* add the coriander and *chillies* (optional). Grind very fine and strain off excess water.

This may be stored in a covered jar in the refrigerator.

When the chutney is to be eaten remove the quantity required and add *lemon juice and salt* to taste.

Coriander leaf chutney goes well with all entree dishes and those main meals which are not curried or heavily spiced.

Liquidised coriander will store well in the refrigerator for a week without the salt and lemon juice.

Halba

Halba is a favourite relish, and this is suggested by the fact that it is widely prepared for Friday night which is the first meal of the Sabbath. It goes well with all the light dishes and is used in much the same way as tomato ketchup.

Halba freezes well so it may be useful to prepare a large quantity and freeze in smaller containers for future use. It keeps well in the fridge for a few days.

The quantities here make a medium sized bowlful of Halba.

Wash and soak *1 tablespoon of fenugreek seeds* overnight. Use at least *2 cups of cold water* to allow the seeds to swell.

Before preparing Halba, drain the water in which the seeds have been soaked, wash the seeds and put into a high speed liquidiser with *2 ozs coriander leaves and stems.* Add *1 teaspoon of coarsely chopped fresh ginger and chillies to taste.* Cover the liquidiser blades with cold water. Liquidise. Within a couple of minutes there should be a fairly thick frothy mixture. Just before serving add *salt* and *lemon juice to taste.* To start with use the juice of *2 lemons* and *2 teaspoons of salt* but add more if preferred. A few teaspoons of cold water may be added for a thinner consistency and this should be beaten well into the mixture.

Traditionally, the soaked seeds and the coriander leaves were ground. Water would be added in small amounts and beaten gradually into the mixture.

Mango & Mint Chutney

The mangoes used for chutney are of the small, green, sour variety. These cooking mangoes are widely available in most Indian greengrocery shops during several months in the year as they are imported from India and East Africa. The Indian variety, which is available during April and May is usually sharper than that imported from East Africa.

If a liquidiser is to be used, pour in enough water to just cover the blades. Add the flesh of *1 lb mangoes* (discard the soft seed in the centre) sliced small and fine. *1 tablespoon of mint leaves* (preferably fresh), *1 teaspoon salt and one or two chopped chillies* (optional). Liquidise for a couple of minutes and serve.

Mango and mint chutney will keep well in the refrigerator, covered, for at least a week.

If a liquidiser is not available, crush the ingredients in a mortar with a pestle.

Some families prefer a mixture of mango and coriander leaves to the mango and mint.

Tomato Sauce

Wash and dry *3 lbs ripe tomatoes.* Boil in *1 cup of malt vinegar and 2 teaspoons tamarind paste.*

When the tomatoes are reduced to pulp, put the mixture through a sieve and add *1 dessertspoon grated ginger, 1 dessertspoon grated garlic, 1$\frac{1}{2}$ teaspoons salt, 1 dessertspoon sugar and 1 dessertspoon of vegetable oil.* Chillies are optional.
Bring the mixture to the boil, reduce the heat and stir until the mixture thickens. Cool and serve cold.
Tomato sauce goes well with all foods with which one would use tomato ketchup.

Aubergine Achaar

For those who like their vegetables pickled in vinegar with hot spices, this variety makes an interesting change.
Bring *2 $\frac{1}{2}$ bottles of malt vinegar* to the boil (560 ml or 20 oz size). When it has boiled, reduce heat and add—

$\frac{1}{4}$ litre of vegetable or sunflower oil

1$\frac{1}{2}$ bottles of vindaloo curry paste (standard size bottle)

1 tablespoon cumin powder

1$\frac{1}{2}$ tablespoons chillie powder (or to taste)

1 dessertspoon garlic powder or freshly grated garlic

1 tablespoon salt

2$\frac{1}{2}$ cups of granulated sugar

Keep this on the boil for half an hour, stirring from time to time.
In the meantime wash and dry *3 lbs of aubergine.* It is essential that the vegetable should be bone dry or else the pickle will mould. It should keep well for a few years if stored in a cool place.
Wash and dry *1 oz green chillies (or to taste).* Make sure the chillies are quite dry, and cut off the stalks.
Add the aubergine and chillies to the boiling vinegar and spices. Boil and then simmer for 15 minutes, stirring from time to time.
Bottle in jars when the mixture is quite cold.
Although the achaar will be ready to eat at this stage it will mature and improve over time.

Bamboo Pickle

Bamboo shoots canned in brine is available in most Indian grocery shops. Cut *3 lbs of bamboo shoots* into thin slices, cover with water and boil for half an hour and drain. Boil *4 pints of malt vinegar and stir in 2 tablespoons of salt and 1 lb of sugar.* Cool. Add *2 cloves of garlic left whole, 2 tablespoons sliced ginger and 1 oz of green chillies* slit down one side. Boil again, then add the bamboo shoots and simmer for a quarter of an hour.

Decant into cold bottles when the mixture is quite cold, ensuring that the level of the vinegar is higher than that of the solid ingredients.

Leave to stand for at least two weeks in a dry, cool place. The longer it is left the more it will mature.

This relish goes well with most fried foods and with meat and poultry which has been grilled or roasted.

Pickled Bamia
(Lady's Fingers)

Wash and dry thoroughly *2 ozs green chillies and 1 lb lady's fingers.* Remove the tops of the lady's fingers and slit down one side to check for and discard imperfect ones.

Meanwhile boil enough malt vinegar to cover the lady's fingers and chillies generously. Season with *1 dessertspoon finely chopped ginger, 1 dessertspoon parsley, 1 dessertspoon salt and 2 dessertspoons sugar.* Add the chillies and lady's fingers, bring to the boil and simmer for 2 minutes. Cool.

When quite cold decant into cold sterile jars and store in a cool place.

Pickled Chillies

This is very useful to have in store in case some members of the family may not like hot food while others do. Those who like it can have chillies on tap prepared in this way. Wash and dry thoroughly *8 ozs of green chillies.* Allow to sweat in *4 tablespoons of vegetable oil* for 5 minutes over a low heat.

Meanwhile boil enough malt vinegar to cover the chilles generously. *Add 1 teaspoon salt and 2 teaspoons of sugar.* Pour in the chillies and oil and bring to the boil, then simmer for 5 minutes. Cool.

When quite cold decant into a large sterile jar. It will keep for months if stored in a cool place.

Chukla Buckla

I believe this means "a mixture" and in this case it is a mixture of vegetables pickled in vinegar.

Wash, dry and break into florettes *1 large cauliflower,* slice *1 lb green beans* (french or bobby beans would be ideal), *1 lb carrots* scrubbed and cut into roughly half inch rings and *2 ozs of green chillies.* Set aside. Chillies are optional for some, essential for others and how much you use will depend on your taste.

Boil *2 pints of vinegar* and season with *1 teaspoon salt,* $\frac{1}{2}$ *teaspoon turmeric and 1 teaspoon finely chopped ginger.* Add the vegetables and boil for 10 minutes. When cold decant into large sterile cold jars making sure that the vegetables are entirely covered with vinegar.

Store in a warm place (on a window sill over a radiator or in an airing cupboard) for at least 3 weeks to mature. This relish will then be ready to eat with light meals, serve as a taster with main meals, or for those who enjoy sharp food — just by itself. The longer Chukla Buckla is stored the more it matures and the better the taste.

Chukla Bukla Achaar

This mixture of vegetables is pickled in oil, vinegar and hot spices.

Wash and dry thoroughly *1 lb of small turnips, 1 cauliflower* cut into florettes, *1 lb carrots* cut into half inch rings and *2 ozs green chillies* (or to taste). It is very important that the vegetables should be bone dry; if not they will mould. Perfectionists wash the vegetables and dry them, leaving them to air overnight to ensure there is no moisture on the surface.

Bring 2 ½ bottles of malt vinegar to the boil (560 ml or 20 oz size). Simmer and season with—

¼ litre of vegetable, sunflower or corn oil

1 ½ bottles of vindaloo curry paste (standard size)

2 cups granulated sugar

1 tablespoon salt

2 teaspoons cumin powder

1 teaspoon turmeric powder

1 teaspoon mustard powder

2 teaspoons chillie powder (or to taste)

Stir and allow to simmer for half an hour.

Add one vegetable at a time, ensuring that it remains on the boil.

Keep boiling for a quarter of an hour, stirring from time to time. Cool.

When the mixture is quite cold bottle in sterile jars. Although the achaar will be edible once it is cooked it will improve over time as it matures and if stored in a cool place will last for years.

Kashmiri Chutney

This is a particular favourite. It is not only eaten as an appetiser but also as a sandwich filling. Mixed with boiled potatoes, and sometimes with an additional layer of sliced cold chicken, it makes a substantial light meal.

Bring *3 bottles of malt vinegar to the boil. (20 oz, 560 ml)* and add *3 tablespoons of tamarind paste.* Stir until the tamarind has dissolved then cool the liquid completely.

Grate 3 lbs of green, cooking mangoes. (The flesh rather than the whole mangoes with the skins should weigh 3 lbs). *Add 1 lb of finely chopped raisins.*

Mix the grated mangoes and raisins with $\frac{1}{2}$ *lb of black mustard seeds,* $\frac{1}{2}$ *lb of garlic, 1 lb of sugar,* $\frac{1}{2}$ *lb of salt and* $\frac{1}{4}$ *lb of ground red chillies (or to taste).*

All the dry ingredients should be added to the cold tamarind and vinegar and stirred thoroughly.

Decant into cold bottles.

The chutney should be allowed to mature for at least six weeks before it is ready to eat.

Pickled Lime or Lemons

Since limes were available in India rather than lemons, lime is the authentic fruit for this recipe. Lemons may be used in just the same way but they are not quite as sharp as limes.

Grate or zest the peels of the required number of *limes — as many as will fit into the glass jar* which is to be used for storage. Place them in the jar and cover completely with the *juice of additional limes. Sprinkle lightly with salt.* One teaspoon to each lime should be sufficient.

Store in a warm place such as an airing cupboard for at least eight weeks, or until the limes soften. In India the jars would be placed in direct sunlight.

The shelf life of limes pickled in this way is indefinite.

Lemboo Ka Achaar
(Lime Pickled in Oil)

Cut in half *12 limes* with the skins on, *sprinkle with salt* and let it rest overnight.

Grate *2 tablespoons of ginger, 1 tablespoon of garlic and add it to 1 tablespoon of sugar, 2 tablespoons of tamarind pulp, 1 tablespoon of salt, 2 teaspoons of turmeric powder.*

Pour *1 pint of vegetable oil* into a large pan and turn on a high flame until the oil begins to smoke. Add all the seasoning, turn down the flame and stir continually until the aroma rises. Turn off the heat as the limes must not be cooked.

Add the lime and all the juices from the lime to the fried spices. Add *1 tablespoon of black mustard seeds* (do not use the yellow variety which is bitter).

When the mixture is cold decant into a glass jar and store for at least two weeks. This pickle has an indefinite shelf life.

Lemboo Basra

This is lime which has been allowed to dry out slowly in a warm place and used to add a sharp edge to certain foods — such as Pilaw Matabakh and the range of Khuttas.

Hang the required number of limes in a piece of nylon netting in an airing cupboard or above a radiator, for several weeks. The limes will gradually dry and become brown When they are completely dry they may be bottled and used as required by crushing the amount of the lime wanted.

Lemboo Basra is common throughout the Middle East, but the name differs slightly from region to region.

Mangoes in Brine

The small, green, cooking mangoes are used for pickling in brine with chillies.

The mangoes should be peeled, cut in half, and washed. The seed should be removed and the mangoes placed in a large jar. For *every pound of mangoes* add *a quarter of c pound of green chillies* (this can be adjusted to taste). For every pound of mango flesh add *a pint of cold water,* and to each pint of water add *1 dessertspoon of salt.*

Cover the jar (s) and store in a warm place for three weeks when the mangoes will soften and mature.

Mango Slice Chutney
(Sweet)

Peel, slice and wash *3 lbs of green cooking mangoes.* Chop *1 tablespoon of garlic, 1 tablespoon of fresh ginger.* Bring *2 bottles of malt vinegar (20 oz, 560 ml)* to the boil. Add the mangoes, garlic and ginger together with *1 tablespoon of onion seeds and 1 tablespoon of salt.* Simmer until the mangoes are just beginning to soften, stirring from time to time. Then add *2 cups of sugar.* Stir constantly until it dissolves. Continue to simmer until the mangoes are cooked through. As an optional extra add *3 tablespoons of raisins and 2 tablespoons of blanched and slivered almonds.* Mix thoroughly.
Cool overnight and decant into cold bottles.
Store in a cool place for an indefinite shelf life.

Turnips & Beetroot in Brine

Use small, tender turnips and beetroot.
Peel the vegetables, and if they are small leave them whole, otherwise chop into mouth-sized pieces. For *every pound of turnips and beetroot add a quarter of a pound of green chillies* (or adjusted to taste). For every pound of turnips and beetroot add *a pint of cold water,* and to each pint of water add *1 dessertspoon of salt .*
Cover the jars and store in a warm place for at least four weeks when the vegetables will soften and mature.

Pickled White Cabbage

Shred *a small to medium sized white cabbage* very fine. Sprinkle with *2 teaspoons of salt.* Allow this to rest for three to four hours or until the cabbage begins to sweat. Drain off the liquid.

Bring *1 pint of malt vinegar* to the boil. Pour over the shredded cabbage together with *2 dessertspoons of finely chopped fresh ginger; 2 ozs. chopped parsley* (Greek parsley is nearer to the leaf used traditionally-'madanus') and *chillies, either green or red, to taste.*

Mix thoroughly and when quite cold decant into large jars, making sure the cabbage is entirely covered with the vinegar. Allow to stand for at least three weeks, preferably in a warm place, to mature.

This relish, like most others, goes well with entree dishes and remains preserved for very long periods provided the ingredients are all well covered with vinegar.

Fish Parra

This is an uncooked pickled fish, usually made in very large quantities and preserved in vinegar. Small quantities were decanted when ready to use and then cooked and eaten with hot boiled rice. A small quantity is suggested here and this can be built up according to requirements.

Buy *3 lbs of salted fish* and set aside. Then mix the following ingredients -

$\frac{3}{4}$ *pint of vegetable oil*
$\frac{1}{2}$ *pint of vinegar*
3 teaspoons chillie powder
3 teaspoons of grated ginger
1$\frac{1}{2}$ teaspoons of grated garlic
2 teaspoons of turmeric
1 teaspoon yellow mustard seeds

Pour a little of the spiced liquid over the bottom of the storage jar and lay down a thin layer of the salted fish, pour more liquid and then another layer of fish until all the ingredients have been stored and spiced evenly. Make sure the liquid covers the fish entirely. Seal and store in a cool place and allow four to six weeks to mature.

When the parra is to be used, pour the portions needed in a saucepan and bring to the boil, then simmer and stir gently for five minutes.

Serve hot with boiled rice. The parra is strong so that a very small quantity is usually eaten in one portion.

Fish Pickle

This pickle is usually made with pomfrets which is a flat fish and now available at many fishmongers or in Bangladeshi shops where frozen fish from the Bay of Bengal is sold.

Use *two large or four small pomfrets*. Scrape the scales with a sharp knife, wash the fish and cut into one inch thick pieces lengthwise and again into two inch thick pieces breadthwise. *Sprinkle with 1 tablespoon of salt and 1 teaspoon of turmeric powder.* Let it rest for a quarter of an hour after which the fish should be dabbed dry with a paper towel. Grate *10 cloves of garlic, 1 teaspoon of fresh root ginger, 3 green chillies* to which *1 tablespoon of fresh coriander leaves should be added.* Rub this paste into the pomfret pieces and sprinkle with *the juice of 1 lemon.* Deep fry the fish in hot oil until golden brown, drain, cool, and set aside.

Dampen *8 oz of dessicated coconut* with just enough water to moisten it so that it resembles the texture of fresh coconut. Place this in a pan over moderate heat and stir continually until it turns golden brown.

In a small frying pan heat *3 tablespoons of vegetable oil.* When it begins to smoke fry $\frac{1}{4}$ *lb of fresh ginger chopped fine,* $\frac{1}{4}$ *lb of garlic* cut in slivers, *2 oz green chillies* slit down one side. Add this to the coconut together with *2 tablespoons of chopped fresh coriander leaves, 4 teaspoons of cinnamon powder, 2 teaspoons of cumin powder and 1 teaspoon pepper.*

Heat $\frac{3}{4}$ *pint of vegetable oil and add 1 teaspoon of black mustard seeds and 1 teaspoon of onion seeds (Koolonji).* When the mustard seeds pop turn off the heat and pour the oil and spices over the coconut mixture. Add *3 tablespoons chillie powder* (or to taste), *4 tablespoons coriander seed powder, 2 teaspoons turmeric powder and salt* (to taste). Mix thoroughly. Add the fish to the mixture and work it through the coconut and spices gently but thoroughly.

When the pickled fish is cold add the juice of *5 lemons* (or to taste) and store in glass jars.

Tickya

This is a very popular savoury which is made from a golden-brown sour plum available in India in winter. I have seen these plums on sale in London in and around greengrocery shops in Brick Lane and Drummond Street, but they have not been as large or as fleshy as those available in India.

Boil *5 lbs of plums in 2 ½ pints of cold water.* Simmer until the plums are reduced to pulp. Remove the skin and stones by forcing the pulp through a coarse sieve. Bring the pulp to the boil again and then simmer until it thickens to a sauce-like consistency. The pulp will need to be stirred from time to time, particularly as it begins to thicken. Add *1 teaspoon of sugar to each pound of pulp.* Add *chillie powder* and *salt* to taste and adjust the sugar. Some people prefer a sweet-sour Tickya, others like it very hot and salty.

Line baking trays with non-stick paper and pour a tablespoon of the sauce at short intervals. Place in an open oven on the lowest light to dry out overnight. In India the sauce was spooned out on large muslin sheets and dried in the direct sun. When the circles of sauce have dried out, peel away from the baking paper and store in an airtight container. Tickya has a very long shelf life if it is properly stored. It is eaten as a tit-bit or 'nosh'.

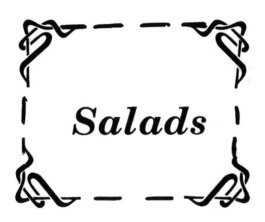

Salads

Vegetable and fruit vendors call at the home of regular customers

Salads

The salads here may be served partly as relishes, on a side plate with the main meal (light or substantial) and partly as small meals in their own right. However, it is very much a matter for individual taste and preference how these foods should be eaten.

Aloomakalla and Mixed Salad

In many households extra aloomakallas (see below) were cooked on Fridays to provide salads for lunch on Saturdays. This recipe is from Bombay.

Chop coarsely *8 cold aloomakallas* and *1 breast of cold chicken.* Chop fine, *2 - 3 raw green mangoes, 2 large carrots, 2 sticks of celery with the leaves, 1 tablespoon of spring onions with the green shoots, 2 green chillies,* and *salt and pepper to taste.* Mix thoroughly and serve.

Cold Chicken Salad

Cut a *breast of chicken* into mouth sized pieces and heap in the centre of a large platter. This could be from Chicken Harikebab (see below) or roast chicken.

Surround the chicken with a wall of mashed *potatoes* cooked in the Harikebab or simply boil the required potatoes and add salt and *a little oil* to moisten.

Arrange in a circle, around the potatoes, boiled *beetroot* cut in fairly thick slices.

Surround the beetroot with sliced *cucumber.*

Surround the cucumber with sliced *tomatoes.*

Surround the sliced tomatoes with coarsely grated *carrots.*

Boil *two or three eggs.* When the eggs are hard, shell them and dip into cold water. Surround the sliced egg whites against the carrots.

Mix the *egg yolks* with *lemon juice and sugar* to taste. It should have the consistency of a stiff paste. Spread widely over vegetables.

Chicken & Mint Salad

This is a popular dish for lunch on Saturdays. It is made from cold Harikebab chicken and potatoes or chicken and cold aloomakalla.

Cut the **chicken pieces and potatoes** into mouth sized pieces. Add **chopped mint leaves,** a little **lemon juice** and **chopped green chillies** to taste.

Mix thoroughly and serve.

Fish Salad - Sardina

This salad from Bombay is a popular cold dish for lunch on Saturdays.

Flake **1 lb of fried white fish** when it is cold. Add **2 or 3 raw green mangoes** chopped fine and **1 tablespoon of spring onions** also chopped fine. Add **salt, pepper and fresh green chillies to taste.** Mix thoroughly and serve.

Onion Salad

Peel the required number of **large onions** and slice across into rings. Sprinkle **salt and** **lemon juice** to taste and a pinch of **cayenne pepper.**

Serve with other salads on a side dish with main meals or rice dishes.

Tomato Salad

This salad is particularly popular. In our household it was made in two ways; the first was called "Pucca" Tomato Salad, ie cooked tomatoes, and this extra effort was made for Friday night and festival meals. Otherwise, we had "Kuccha" Tomato Salad, when the tomatoes were left uncooked.

For the "Pucca" Salad boil *1 lb fresh tomatoes* in enough cold water to cover them. When the skins begin to crack, remove from the water and cool. Place each tomato on a board, remove the skin and discard, and crush the flesh with a fork. (Otherwise the tomatoes may be put through a coarse sieve).

Add the *juice of half a lemon, $\frac{1}{2}$ teaspoon of salt (or to taste), 1 tablespoon finely chopped coriander leaves, 1 tablespoon of finely chopped spring onions and 1 green chillie* (optional).

Mix thoroughly and serve with light meals, with pilaw or main meals.

For the "Kuccha" Tomato Salad chop the fresh tomatoes instead of boiling. All the other ingredients remain the same.

Tomato and Cucumber Salad

Wash and dry *1 lb of fresh tomatoes* and chop fine. Peel *half a cucumber,* chop fine and add it to the tomatoes. Slice *1 oz of spring onions including the green shoots* and add to the tomatoes and cucumber. Chop *1 tablespoon of fresh coriander leaves* and add it to the salad. Sprinkle with *the juice of half a lemon and salt to taste.* Mix thoroughly and allow to stand for at least an hour before serving, preferably in the refrigerator.

Zalatta

Peel and slice as finely as possible *1 cucumber* (or *1 lb small cucumbers* such as those imported from Cyprus). Sprinkle with *2 teaspoons of salt* and allow to sweat for an hour. Squeeze dry and cover with *malt vinegar;* add *1 teaspoon coarsely chopped ginger, 1 dessertspoon parsley* (preferably Greek parsley, sometimes called 'madanus') and *1 chopped green chillie* (optional). Rest for at least an hour. Zalatta has a long shelf life, stored in a cool place, provided the ingredients remain covered with vinegar.

Soups & Stews

Planning vegetarian meals

Soups and Stews

The dishes in this section cover a range of soups, stews and ragouts. Traditionally they are eaten with either rice or pilaw as complete meals. Some of the soups or stews are suitable as starters but the range of khattas, or sweet-sour ragouts combined with chicken should be served the traditional way.

Although the chickens in these recipes are cooked by boiling, I prefer to use roasters. The cooking times are for roasters in all cases and longer cooking times will be necessary for boiling fowls.

All the dishes in this section are boiled. Once all the ingredients have been mixed, covered with water and brought to the boil, the cooking is completed by simmering. As a general rule the lid should be left on the saucepan when simmering.

Beetroot Soup

This is a simple and delicious cold soup and is most refreshing on a hot day.

Peel and quarter *five medium sized beetroots.* Bring to the boil with *2 pints of cold water.* Simmer until the beetroot is tender. Add the juice of *1 lemon and sugar to taste* when the liquid is quite cold.

Refrigerate and serve in bowls, about 1 beetroot and a ladleful of liquid for each person.

Dal Soup

This is a very popular food throughout India but since lentil soups, or soups with lentils are well known in the Middle East, the recipe will be included here.

Pick over and wash thoroughly *1 cup of red lentils*. Cover this with *1 cup of boiling water* and keep on the boil. Slice *a small onion* and add this to the lentils. Simmer until the lentils have broken down, which should take about a quarter of an hour. Stir hard or whisk so that the lentils and water become thoroughly integrated. Then add $\frac{1}{2}$ *tea cup of cold water* which will give the liquid a smooth consistency. Continue to simmer.

Meanwhile heat *2 teaspoons of cumin powder, 2 grated cloves of garlic and 1 teaspoon of salt in 2 tablespoons of vegetable oil* over a moderately high flame. When the oil begins to smoke and the aroma of the garlic and cumin rises, add this very gradually and carefully to the lentils. Care must be taken because the oil bubbles when poured into the lentils. Stir vigorously or whisk and then *add salt*.

Serve very hot with boiled rice. This is the traditional way to eat dal. However, if it is to be used as a starter, one way to serve it is without rice but with diced raw vegetables such as peppers, celery and carrot. Although untraditional, it is delicious and nutritious eaten this way.

Vegetable Soup

This vegetable soup is a good starter either with the vegetables served whole or liquidised. Traditionally it is eaten in the former way with a few spoons of rice.

Saute *1 large onion* finely sliced in *3 tablespoons of vegetable oil*. When the onions are glazed add and blend in *1 lb of chopped fresh or canned tomatoes (with the liquid)*. Simmer until the mixture has the consistency of a puree and the tomatoes are cooked through.

Add *2 pints of cold water* and bring to the boil. Then add the vegetables. These are a matter of choice and can be varied, but a good traditional combination would be *1 large carrot diced, 2 large potatoes quartered, 3 ozs fresh or frozen peas, 2 ozs sliced green beans, fresh or frozen, 1 small marrow or 2 peeled and sliced courgettes.*

Bring to the boil and simmer until the vegetables are tender but crisp.

Add *2 tablespoons fresh chopped coriander leaves (optional), salt and pepper to taste.*

Just before serving add the *juice of 1 lemon.*

Serve hot.

Egjosh

This is a fish soup which could be used as an entree dish, or served with boiled rice could provide a main meal.

Saute *2 large onions* sliced very fine in *4 tablespoons of vegetable or corn oil.* When the onions are tender and thoroughly glazed, add *1 teaspoon of turmeric powder, 2 teaspoons of salt and pepper to taste.* If you enjoy chillies then add one or two at this stage.

Add *2 pints of cold water* for *four to six portions of fish* and bring to the boil. White fish is best - haddock or cod would be ideal; fillet the fish or cut in portions on the bone, wash and put into the pot to boil. It is best to leave the skin on while cooking to prevent the flesh breaking up.

When on the boil add *several sprigs of fresh coriander leaves.* In Bombay it was customary to add $\frac{1}{2}$ *teaspoon of 'Panchforan'.* (This is a mixture of 5 spices).

Simmer until the fish is just cooked through. Remove the fish, skin and return to the soup. It is very easy to skin fish while it is still hot.

Just before serving, add the *juice of 1 lemon.*

Serve on a bed of hot rice.

Fish Khutta With Koobas

Chop *a medium sized onion* and glaze in *3 tablespoons of vegetable oil .* Add *8 ozs of chopped fresh or tinned tomatoes,* $\frac{1}{2}$ *teaspoon of sugar, 1 teaspoon salt, pepper to taste,* $\frac{1}{4}$ *teaspoon turmeric.* Bring this to the boil, mixing thoroughly and then simmer until the tomatoes and onions are reduced to a smooth sauce. Add *a pint of cold water,* bring to the boil and simmer.

For stuffing koobas take *1 lb of minced white fish.* Chop *a large onion,* sprinkle with *1 teaspoon of salt* and let it stand for a quarter of an hour. Squeeze the onions dry, and add this to the fish with *1 teaspoon chopped parsley* or mint, *1 teaspoon grated ginger or ginger powder, 1 teaspoon grated garlic,* $\frac{1}{2}$ *teaspoon salt and pepper to taste,* and mix thoroughly.

For the coating, take $\frac{1}{2}$ *lb of fine rice flour, a pinch of salt, 1 teaspoon of the fish mixture* **and add** *enough cold water* to make a firm dough. Flatten a tablespoon of the rice flour mixture in the palm of one hand. Place a heaped teaspoon of the stuffing in the middle and work the rice flour casing around it until it is sealed. The casing should be neither very thin nor very thick.

When the koobas are made, lower gently into the boiling tomato and onion sauce. When the koobas are firm move them around gently to make sure they do not stick to the bottom of the saucepan. Simmer the koobas for 20 minutes.

Serve hot with boiled rice, pilaw or boiled potatoes.

Talpechal

This fish soup was prepared by most families in Cochin every day for lunch excep Saturday. It was probably as popular there as chicken soup or murug was for the Jewish community in Calcutta.

Grate *1 large onion, 3 cloves of garlic and $\frac{1}{2}$ teaspoon of fresh root ginger and fry in 3 tablespoons of vegetable oil.* [Coconut oil was generally used in Cochin but this has a strong flavour and may be substituted with other vegetable or seed oils.] When the onions are glazed add *1 oz of fresh or dried curry leaves, 1 teaspoon coriander powder and 4 ozs of chopped fresh tomatoes* or *2 ozs tomato puree.* Stir until the tomatoes have cooked through. Add *1 $\frac{1}{2}$ pints of cold water* and bring to the boil. Add *2 lbs of fish o* your choice, bring to the boil once more and simmer gently until the fish has cooked through. Add *vinegar, salt and pepper* to taste.

Unjuly

This is a coconut-based cold fish soup, easy to prepare, and is refreshing on a warm day.

Wash *4 good sized cutlets from white fish,* dry, sprinkle with *a teaspoon of salt and $\frac{1}{2}$ teaspoon of turmeric.* Allow the fish to stand for about fifteen minutes. Pat dry with a paper towel, coat lightly with *plain flour,* and fry in *vegetable oil.* Set aside.

Dissolve a *7 oz cake of cream of coconut* in *1 $\frac{1}{2}$ pints of water.* Bring this to the boil and simmer until the cream has dissolved. Add *2 tablespoons of chopped fresh coriander leaves, 2 tablespoons of chopped spring onions, and 2 chopped fresh green chillies* (optional). The chillies may be substituted by sweet green peppers. One tablespoon would be sufficient. Season with *1 teaspoon of salt and pepper* to taste. Add the *juice of 1 lemon* or *$\frac{1}{2}$ cup of cider vinegar.*

Pour the soup over the pieces of fried fish, cool and refrigerate. Serve cold. Unjuly is sometimes eaten with boiled white rice, but more often it is served without supplementary foods.

Fatooth

Fatooth has a soup base, cooked with only breast of chicken, pieces of bread of a special kind called "Sayeed" bread in Calcutta, and Halba.

I have not seen "Sayeed" bread in England. It does not become soggy and disintegrate when dunked in soup. This yeast bread is rolled fine, and baked in a "Tandoor" which is an open clay oven in which the bread is baked very quickly against the inner walls. The bread is fairly crisp, except at the outer edges, which remain soft.

Proceed by using the recipe for Murug (see below), using only breast of chicken. The chicken is cut into chunks, and the Sayeed bread broken into pieces and immersed in the soup. Finally each portion is topped with Halba when served individually.

Khutta

Khutta is the generic name of a sweet-sour ragout. This may be prepared with vegetables only ; with vegetables and koobas (kooftas ie chicken or meat balls covered with rice dough), or vegetables and chicken pieces.

The common basis : Stir fry *1 medium sized chopped onion, 1 teaspoon grated ginger (or ginger powder) and $\frac{1}{2}$ teaspoon grated garlic.* Add *1 teaspoon salt, pepper to taste and a generous pinch of turmeric.* When the onions are glazed (they should not be browned) add *1 $\frac{1}{2}$ pints of cold water* and bring to the boil.

Vegetables which are suitable for khutta are beetroot, carrots and lady's fingers. The hard vegetables such as beetroot and carrot may be added at this stage. Either use *1 lb of sliced raw beetroot* or *1 lb of chopped carrots,* and *8 ozs chopped tomatoes.* Add to the cold water mixture and bring to the boil. Then simmer for 15 minutes. The tomatoes are optional but enhance the lady's fingers particularly.

In the meantine make the koobas. Start by making kooftas.

CHICKEN OR MEAT KOOBAS

For the kooftas, take the $\frac{1}{2}$ *chicken breast which has been minced, 1 teaspoon chopped parsley, mint or celery leaves, 1 teaspoon grated ginger or ginger powder, 1 teaspoon grated garlic, 1 small grated onion, $\frac{1}{4}$ teaspoon turmeric, $\frac{1}{2}$ teaspoon salt, pepper to taste.* Mix thoroughly to the consistency of a soft dough. To encase the kooftas and make koobas, take $\frac{1}{2}$ *lb of rice flour, a pinch of salt, 1 teaspoon of the koofta mixture* and add *enough cold water* to make a very firm but pliable dough. The koobas should be roughly the size of small walnuts. Flatten a tablespoon of the rice flour mixture in the palm of your hands. Place a heaped teaspoon of the koofta mixture in the middle and work the rice flour case around it until it is sealed. The rice flour case should not be too thin or else it will break up while cooking, nor should it be too thick, or the result will be stodgy.

As each kooba is ready, gently lower into the simmering liquid. Once the koobas firm up move them around gently to ensure they do not stick to the bottom of the saucepan. Cook the koobas for 15 minutes. The above quantities should produce 12 koobas.

VEGETABLE KOOBAS

Make the kooftas with $\frac{1}{4}$ *lb of peas,* $\frac{1}{4}$ *lb chopped beans* (any green variety will be suitable) and $\frac{1}{4}$ *lb chopped carrots.* Boil the vegetables until they are tender. Chop *a small onion,* sprinkle with salt and allow this to stand for about ten minutes. This will tenderise the onions. Mix with the other vegetables. Add $\frac{1}{4}$ *teaspoon turmeric,* $\frac{1}{2}$ *teaspoon salt and pepper to taste, 1 teaspoon chopped parsley, mint or celery leaves, 1 teaspoon grated ginger or ginger powder and 1 teaspoon grated garlic.* Mix thoroughly and form into little balls, the size of small walnuts. Encase these kooftas in the dough made with rice flour as shown above for the chicken or meat koobas.

If lady's finger khutta is being prepared, top and tail *1 lb of lady's fingers* and slit the vegetable down one side to ensure there are no parasites. Wash and add to the simmering liquid once the koobas begin to firm up. This delicate vegetable should not be overcooked, but remain firm and whole.

KHUTTA WITH CHICKEN

Follow the instructions on the common basis shown above. Add the chicken pieces together with the vegetables, bring to the boil and simmer until the chicken pieces are tender. For lady's fingers add the vegetable when the chicken pieces are almost cooked through.

About five minutes before serving, add *1 or 2 tablespoons chopped mint, the juice of 1 large lemon and 1 tablespoon of sugar.* Stir thoroughly.

Serve hot. The range of khuttas is generally eaten with pilaw or boiled rice.

FISH AND LADY'S FINGER KHUTTA

Follow the instructions on the common basis shown above. Add pieces of fish which have been fried until golden and set aside, simmer in the stew for ten minutes, then add *1 or 2 tablespoons of chopped mint, the juice of a large lemon and 1 tablespoon of sugar.* Allow to simmer for a further five minutes and serve hot.

An alternative and easier method is to prepare the lady's finger khutta, add small fish fillets and allow to simmer until they are almost cooked through. Then add the mint, lemon juice and sugar as above.

Mahmoora

Mahmoora is also a ragout and is a variant on Khutta. These sweet-sour ragouts are of Middle Eastern origin.

Chop *a small onion* and saute in *1 tablespoon of vegetable oil.* When the onion is glazed add *a teaspoon of grated ginger, 2 or 3 cloves of grated garlic, $\frac{1}{2}$ teaspoon turmeric, 1 teaspoon of salt and pepper to taste.* Stir fry. Add the pieces of a jointed *chicken about 4 $\frac{1}{2}$ lbs weight.* Pour on $\frac{1}{2}$ *cup of cold water.* Stir over a high flame until the mixture comes to the boil, reduce to a medium flame, cover and cook for fifteen minutes by which time the liquid should be almost completely reduced.

In the meantime blanch about *12 almonds,* skin, and split in halves. Wash **1 oz of raisins.** *Cut four cloves of garlic* into slivers (optional). Add these ingredients to the reduced chicken, cover entirely with cold water and bring to the boil. Then simmer until the chicken is tender.

Five minutes before serving add *1 tablespoon chopped fresh mint leaves, 1 tablespoon of sugar* and either *the juice of 1 lemon or 2 teaspoons of tamarind paste.*
Serve hot with pilaw or boiled rice.

Murug

Chicken soup is a great favourite among all Jewish communities although there are considerable differences between East and West. The basic way to make Murug would probably still produce a soup, but when it is elaborated, for tomato murug or vegetable murug the appearance and taste alters substantially and they are more correctly stews.

Murug may be served as an elaborate first course; traditionally it is eaten with rice and makes a complete and substantial meal.

Prepare a *5 lb roasting chicken* by jointing, washing and removing the skin to avoid unwanted fat. Set aside.

Slice *a small onion,* add *1 or 2 crushed cloves of garlic* and *1 teaspoon of chopped or grated fresh ginger.* This should be stir fried with *1 tablespoon of vegetable oil* in a deep saucepan. Add *1 teaspoon of turmeric powder, 1 cardimum pod and salt and pepper to taste and $\frac{1}{2}$ pint cold water.* When the above mixture has been cooked and reduced add the chicken pieces and seal over a hot flame. Stir thoroughly, cover and cook for 15 minutes until the juices are absorbed into the chicken. Peel and halve *potatoes as required* (this is optional), add *2 $\frac{1}{2}$ pints of cold water* and bring to the boil. Simmer until the chicken is tender. This should take about 45 minutes.

For TOMATO MURUG add *1 lb chopped fresh, ripe tomatoes* or a can of chopped tomatoes or 2 ozs of tomato puree, after the chicken has been sealed. Make sure the tomatoes are mixed in thoroughly.

For VEGETABLE MURUG in addition to the tomatoes add *one chopped carrot, 2 peeled and sliced courgettes (or pieces of marrow when in season), 2 ozs sliced beans, 2 ozs peas* after the chicken has been sealed.

Serve hot with rice.

Murug Arook

This dish is a little time-consuming to prepare and used to be served on special feast days in our home. For those who enjoy the flavour of spring onions and fresh coriander leaves, Murug Arook will be a great favourite.

Prepare *chicken stock,* or for those who are content to use a concentrated chicken soup cube, use *2 cubes and 3 pints of water.*

Arook is a filling of minced breast of chicken mixed with a number of other ingredients, encased in a coat of rice, spring onions and finely chopped coriander leaves.

To make the filling use *1 lb of minced breast of chicken* and mix with *1 small chopped onion, 2 cloves of grated garlic, 1 teaspoon of grated ginger, $\frac{1}{4}$ teaspoon of turmeric powder, 1 teaspoon salt and pepper to taste, and the juice of half a lemon.* Mix the ingredients thoroughly and divide the mixture into balls - about the size of a large marble.

Use white *Patna* rice for the casing. Wash and bring $\frac{1}{2}$ *lb of Patna rice* to the boil. Continue boiling for another 5 minutes. Strain, but do not drain with water. Chop *6 ozs of spring onions very fine (including the fresh green shoots)* and add to the rice together with *3 tablespoons of fresh coriander leaves* also chopped fine, or ground. Sprinkle with $\frac{1}{2}$ *teaspoon of salt and pepper to taste.* Knead the rice, onions and coriander leaves until it forms a stiff dough. Divide the mixture into portions corresponding to the balls prepared for the filling. There should be 12 Arooks, but this will depend on the size preferred. Wet your hands, take a portion of the casing mixture and flatten in the hollow of your palm. Place a ball of filling in the centre and work around it until it is completely covered and sealed. Set aside on a dish and leave to stand for at least 30 minutes - preferably longer. This will help to firm them up.

Bring the chicken stock to the boil and gently lower the Arooks into it. Simmer for 30 minutes. Boiling on a high light will break up the Arooks.

Serve the Arooks in the Murug (or chicken stock) while piping hot.

No supplementary dishes are served with Murug Arook generally. It is a meal in itself.

Watch points to ensure the Arooks do not break up while cooking -
1. Use a sticky rice, such as Patna, to hold the casing together.
2. Wet your hands after you make each Arook.
3. Let the Arooks rest before they are cooked. Two or three hours would be best.
4. Cook the Arooks on a very low light.

Shorba

In essence, Shorba is a dense stew of rice and shredded chicken. It may be served as a substantial starter although some may consider it sufficient for a main meal with a fresh salad on the side.

Shorba may be prepared by using wings and ribs of chicken together with gizzards.

Wash *4 ozs of white rice* and place in a heavy pan with *1 oz of chicken fat* or 1 tablespoon of vegetable oil. Add *1 small chopped onion, a large pinch of turmeric powder, $\frac{1}{2}$ teaspoon of salt and pepper to taste, $\frac{1}{2}$ teaspoon ginger powder, 1 stick of cinnnamon, 2 cloves and 2 pods of cardimum.* Stir fry until the ingredients are thoroughly mixed. *Add a few chicken pieces and gizzards with half a cup of cold water.* Turn on a high flame and stir until the water is reduced. Pour on *2 pints of cold water,* bring to the boil and simmer for an hour or until the stew is thickened with the rice and the chicken is so tender that it falls off the bones. Remove the bones and serve very hot.

Watch the Shorba as it begins to thicken, and stir frequently to make sure the rice and chicken does not stick to the bottom of the saucepan.

Vegetables Stewed in Meat Stock

This vegetable stew from Cochin is made in stock from beef and chicken bones and would therefore need to be adapted for strict vegetarians.

Boil *1 lb of beef bones and the bones of a chicken* in *2 pints of cold water.* Remove the deposits from the meat which rise to the top in the course of boiling and simmer for an hour. *Add 1 large sliced onion, 1 large chopped carrot, 2 large chopped tomatoes and 3 cloves of crushed garlic.* Simmer for half an hour. Add *2 peeled and halved potatoes, 2 chopped celery stalks, and a marrow cut into wedges.* Bring to the boil and simmer for another half an hour.

Add *1 teaspoon coriander powder, salt and pepper to taste* and boil for another 5 minutes.

Serve hot with rice.

Light   Meals

Vegetables being prepared for cooking by women in the household to make sure there are no parasites, as advocated by Jewish law.

Light Meals

Light and main meals are separated here in a somewhat artifical way, more as a way of fitting into eating styles in the West rather than as an indication of our own tradition. Light meals are suggested here as entree dishes, picnic foods, buffet plates, etc., and also as part of a main meal where suitable.

This section is divided into vegetarian and then non-vegetarian dishes.

Aloomakalla

Every Friday night, every festival, every private celebration where it was usual to prepare a cooked meal, aloomakalla has always been a "must". I have never met anyone, who has not gone overboard for this method of preparing potatoes. The word "aloo" is the Hindi for potatoes and "makalla" is the Arabic for "fried", so that the name itself is hybrid.

Small to medium-sized potatoes should be used for this dish and it is essential that the potatoes should be of the hardest variety available. The potatoes are deep fried slowly for several hours in a "karai" or wok-like utensil. Allow for no less than *four potatoes per person* otherwise there will be disappointed diners, and no less than two hours cooking time.

Peel the *potatoes* and place them in *a saucepan of cold water* with *turmeric and salt to taste.* Parboil the potatoes, drain, cool and pierce each potato once with a fork. Transfer the potatoes into the "karai" and *cover with oil.* Bring to the boil and then simmer until a very pale golden crust is formed on the outside. Move gently from time to time. When the crust is beginning to form all over, the potatoes may be left and the cooking resumed about half an hour before time to serve up. Otherwise continue to simmer the potatoes, turning from time to time until the crust gradually becomes thicker. About five minutes before serving, turn the flame high and continue turning the potatoes until the crust is hard and a golden-brown colour.

Drain the potatoes on kitchen paper to ensure they are "dry" when served. Aloomakalla should not be served floating in oil. The outside should have a crust so hard that it may be difficult to pierce with a knife, while the inside should remain soft.

Serve with roast meat, chicken, duck or turkey. It would also go well with fried fish.

The oil can be used again. Leave one potato in the hot oil when serving so that the oil does not burn. Strain and store for further use.

This is the traditional way to prepare aloomakalla. Shortcuts have been tried and used here quite successfully, although the crust is not as thick as it might be otherwise. For example, the potatoes are not parboiled but put straight into hot oil. When the crust has formed, the potatoes may be put in the oven to harden on a medium to high temperature, eg. gas mark 6.

Fried Aubergine

Fried aubergine is traditionally eaten with fried fish. The aubergine should be washed and the stalk removed, but should not be peeled. Cut each *aubergine* lengthway into *four or five slices, sprinkle with salt* and allow to sweat for 20-30 minutes. Wash and dry each piece, score the surface gently, *salt lightly,* (sprinkle with $\frac{1}{2}$ *teaspoon coriander powder and $\frac{1}{2}$ teaspoon cumin powder optional*) and fry until golden brown Serve hot with fried fish.

This is the traditional method. Now that oven cooking is widely used, the vegetable is not fried but smeared with oil and baked on a medium to high temperature until it is golden brown.

Bhaji

Those familiar with Indian food will know that a bhaji is a dish of vegetables mostly spiced, laced with chillies, and often prepared in a sauce. We have modified this somewhat so that our bhajis are seldom spiced and the vegetables remain crisp and dry rather than in an oily sauce. Bhajis may be eaten as a main meal with boiled rice, pilaw or a range of Indian bread. This would suit vegetarians. Adapted to Western styles of eating, bhajis make an interesting substitute for boiled vegetables when served with meat poultry or fish.

I shall concentrate on a few varieties of bhajis but the options are as wide as the availability of fresh or even frozen vegetables and there is plenty of scope to develop combinations which are best suited to individual tastes.

Traditionally, potatoes are added to other vegetables when cooking most bhaji The potatoes absorb the flavours of the other vegetables and are quite delicious.

Cauliflower Bhaji

Saute a sliced *medium sized onion in 3 tablespoons of vegetable oil.* Add *teaspoon of turmeric powder, 1 teaspoon of salt, pepper to taste.* Stir, and add *florettes *f a medium sized cauliflower* and *4 medium sized potatoes* which have been peeled and ut in quarters. (The potatoes are optional). Blend in thoroughly with the onions.

These are the basic ingredients for a cauliflower bhaji but other vegetables may be dded to make a change. For example, add *8 oz of fresh or tinned tomatoes or 2 ozs *omato puree* or, add *3 oz frozen or fresh peas, 3 oz sliced beans, 1 chopped carrot and *alf a green pepper,* coarsely chopped. These additional vegetables should be added to he sauted onions at the same time as the cauliflower and potatoes.

Mix the vegetables thoroughly, cover, and cook in a preheated oven on gas mark 4 (450°) on the middle shelf for one hour or until the cauliflower is cooked through but emains firm and crisp. Half way through the cooking, stir the vegetables to make sure hey blend while cooking.

Serve hot or cold in one of the ways suggested.

Lady's Finger Bhaji

Saute *a sliced small onion in 3 tablespoons of vegetable oil.* Add $\frac{1}{2}$ *teaspoon of *urmeric, 1 teaspoon salt and pepper to taste.* Add *1 lb of fresh or canned tomatoes* which have been coarsely chopped and blend in thoroughly with the onions. Bring to the boil and then simmer until the tomatoes are cooked through to a fairly smooth onion and omato sauce. Add *1 lb lady's fingers* (known as bamia in Greek-Cypriot shops and bindi n Indian shops. It is also called okra). Remove the top and bottom tips of the vegetables, hen slit down one side from top to bottom to ensure there are no parasites, and wash horoughly.

Mix the vegetables, cover and cook in a preheated oven for one hour on gas mark 4 (450°) on the middle shelf.

Beans Bhaji

String and slice *2 lbs of beans* - any green variety will do. Wash thoroughly. Frozen beans immersed in boiling water for two minutes may be used if preferred. Saute a *medium sized onion in 3 tablespoons of vegetable oil.* Add *1 teaspoon of turmeric, 1 $\frac{1}{2}$ teaspoons of salt and pepper to taste, the beans* and $\frac{1}{2}$ *lb of potatoes* cut in cubes (optional). Blend thoroughly.

Cover, and cook for one hour in a preheated oven on gas mark 4 (450°) on the middle shelf.

Spinach Bhaji

Pick over and wash thoroughly *2 lbs of spinach*. Set aside to drain. Saute *a medium sized sliced onion* in *3 tablespoons of vegetable oil.* Add the spinach and cook on a very low heat for five minutes. Turn the leaves over, cover and cook for another five minutes or until the spinach is cooked through. To add to the flavour, it is possible to include other aromatic leaves, chopped fine with the spinach, such as fenugreek, coriander or Greek parsley. Start with a tablespoon and adjust according to taste.

Aubergine Bhaji

This bhaji requires a little more effort as ideally aubergines should be sliced, lightly salted and left to stand for half an hour before cooking. They should be washed thoroughly to get rid of the bitterness. Prepare *1 ½ lbs of aubergine* in this way. Slice finely *one green, yellow or red pepper.* Blanch, or soak in boiling water for a few minutes. Prepare *1 ½ lbs of courgettes* by removing the top and bottom tips, washing thoroughly and cutting across in ¼ " thick slices (leave the skin on). Shell ¼ *lb of peas* or use frozen peas dipped in boiling water for a couple of minutes. Slice and wash ¼ *lb green beans* or frozen beans dipped in boiling water. Peel and quarter ½ *lb potatoes* (optional).

Having prepared these vegetables, saute *a large sliced onion in 4 tablespoons of vegetable oil.* Add *1 lb tomatoes* - fresh or canned - coarsely chopped. Bring to the boil and simmer until reduced to a fairly smooth sauce. Add *1 teaspoon turmeric, 2 teaspoons salt, pepper to taste.* Add all the prepared vegetables and mix thoroughly.

Cook for an hour in a covered saucepan on gas mark 4 (450°) middle shelf or until the vegetables are cooked through but firm. Half way through the cooking stir well and add *1 tablespoon of fresh coriander leaves* (optional - but for those who enjoy the aroma of this herb - it makes a noticeably welcome difference).

For more unusual bhajis try AAM ALOO (raw mangoes of the cooking variety and potatoes), DRUMSTICKS (available in Indian greengroceries), PEAS, BEANS AND FENUGREEK LEAVES. (Ask for 'maythee sag' in Indian shops).

Bharta

"Bharta" is the Hindi word for "mash". Although this would suggest dishes o
Indian origin, they are more akin to those of the Middle East.

POTATO BHARTA

Boil, skin and mash *4 medium sized potatoes* with a fork. Add the *juice of half a
lemon, 1 tablespoon of spring onions (including the green shoots) and 1 chopped green
chillie* (optional).
Serve with any vegetable, poultry, fish or meat.
Bharta is delicious served hot or cold.

TOMATO BHARTA

Boil, skin and mash *4 medium sized potatoes* with a fork. Boil and skin *2 medium
sized tomatoes* and add the pulp to the potatoes. Add the juice of *half a lemon
1 tablespoon of spring onions and 1 chopped chillie* (optional).
Serve as suggested for Potato Bharta.

BRINJAL OR AUBERGINE BHARTA

Bake *2 medium sized aubergines* in a very hot oven. (Gas mark 8) until the skir
burns off. Wash under a cold tap and squeeze out as much of the juice as possible as thi
is bitter. Slice and mash the aubergine and add the *juice of 1 lemon, 1 chopped green
chillie, 2 tablespoons of spring onions finely chopped, 1 tablespoon of olive oil,* (o
vegetable oil). Season with *1 teaspoon of salt and pepper to taste.*

Serve cold
Aubergine bharta goes particularly well with fried fish but can also be eaten with
meat or poultry.

A tablespoon of finely chopped coriander leaves would go well with any variety o
"bharta".

Cheese

Cheese was not usually prepared in individual homes as there were special suppliers who made it to order. The best known were "Tookra Paneer" which means blocks or pieces of cheese and "Chonti Paneer" or braided cheese. These cheeses are sold by Lebanese merchants in some Western countries.

Tookra Paneer is made with the richest milk available in order to maximise its bulk. This should be warmed to blood heat, i e it should be no hotter than lukewarm, and rennet added as directed. Rennet is available in health food shops specifically for making cheese, and is a vegetable product. I have also used rennet for making junket and the result is equally satisfactory. Within two or three hours the water will have separated out from the bulk of the milk and can be poured through a cheese cloth or fine muslin to drain the water. Twist the cloth to drain off more water, put in a colander in the sink, and place a heavy weight on the cheese. If this is done overnight the cheese should be sufficiently dry by the following morning to transfer to a plate or tray in the shape of a square or oblong block.

Leave the cheese to dry in the air for twenty four hours, and then store in a jar of salt water in the refrigerator. It should keep for three or four weeks. I would suggest *1 teaspoon of salt to a pint of cold water* for storage because in a day or two the cheese absorbs a great deal of salt. Wait for a day, at least, before eating so that the cheese can absorb some salt and mature.

Like others before me in this country, I have had no success with *braided cheese*. This could be because pasturised milk is generally used here whereas it is unpasturised in India. It is also possible that vegetarian rennet does not produce the required result. The recipe will nevertheless be included here if only for the record. Exactly the same method was suggested to me from more than one source which suggests that one of the two ingredients, or both of them, do not produce the results achieved in India.

When the block cheese has been prepared, and before it is immersed in salt water, it should be cut into pieces lengthwise, about 1" thick. Bring enough water to the boil to cover the pieces and then add the cheese. As the water boils, press the pieces together with a long-handled spoon until they coagulate. This should take between five and ten minutes. The boiled cheese should then be placed on a tray and when it is cool enough to handle it should be pressed manually to free the excess water. The cheese should now have an elastic consistency and look as if it consists of many strands. When it is cool it should be made into long rolls and braided. Unfortunately I did not achieve the elasticity necessary for successful braiding. Instead the cheese crumbled. The braided cheese should also be stored in salt water.

Yoghurt Cheese

Prepare the yoghurt first by bringing milk to boiling point. Cool to a temperature of between 43°- 49° C. Stir in the yoghurt culture in the proportion of *1 large teaspoon to a pint of milk.* Seal the warm milk in an insulated container - not with a vacuum. Leave it in the container to set for at least 12 hours. Decant and allow to stand either in or out of the refrigerator for at least another 12 hours for the best flavour.

Place a cheesecloth or fine muslin around the inside of a colander and tip the yoghurt into it. Cover with the cloth and allow it to drain in the sink overnight.

The next morning you should have a fine spreading cheese made from the yoghurt.

The principle is the same for making cream cheese except that cream cheese is made from milk which has been allowed to sour.

Filowrees

Filowrees are not dissimilar from Felafel in Israel and Egypt, except the basic ingredient is split green peas in India whereas it is chick peas in the Middle East.

Filowrees used to be a favourite party food among the Indian Jews, and when it was made in our household the children made a nuisance of themselves, harassing the cook for tasters before the filowrees were out of the frying pan.

Soak *8 oz of split green peas* (called chunna-ka-dal in Indian shops). Preferably, this should be done overnight. The next day the dried peas should be thoroughly washed and crushed in a blender with just enough water to cover the blades. It is important that the paste should be as stiff as possible.

When the paste has been prepared, add *2 oz of finely chopped spring onions, 4 tablespoons of chopped fresh coriander leaves, and 2 teaspoons of whole carraway seeds. Salt* should be added to taste. *Chopped chillies* are optional.

Blend thoroughly. A spoonful of the mixture should be dropped at intervals into a pan of *boiling oil* and deep fried.

When golden brown, remove from the frying pan and drain. Serve hot as a finger food. Filowrees will go splendidly with drinks before supper or could be used as a starter with a green salad.

Mahmoosa

This is an economical vegetarian dish which makes a satisfying light meal. An untraditional, but nevertheless interesting way to serve it would be as part of a main meal, with roast chicken or meat and as an alternative to a conventional way of preparing potatoes.

The first recipe for Mahmoosa is the traditional method and although it may be a little laborious to chop the potatoes fine it is well worth the effort. The second method is simpler and may be more convenient but there is a difference in taste.

Prepared either way, Mahmoosa may be served hot or cold. If it is to be served at a party it may be prepared in advance as it will keep well in the fridge for a few days if it is covered.

For 4 people.

Chop fine *a small to medium sized onion,* and saute in *3 tablespoons of vegetable or sunflower oil.* Meanwhile, peel and cut in half *3 medium to large potatoes.* A soft variety is best. Slice lengthways and then breadthways as finely as possible. The chopped potatoes may be put into a bowl of water while working on them to prevent discolouring. Drain the chopped potatoes, add to the sauted onions and mix thoroughly. Turn the heat high and then simmer, stirring every four or five minutes to ensure the potatoes do not stick to the bottom of the pan. Cook for about 15 minutes, preferably covered, until the chopped potatoes are tender. Then add *4 eggs (size 2),* $\frac{1}{2}$ *teaspoon of turmeric,* $\frac{1}{2}$ *to 2 teaspoons of salt and pepper to taste.* Scramble for 5 minutes until the egg is thoroughly mixed in with the potato. Simmer until the Mahmoosa is dry, turning from time to time. The drying process should take about another 5 minutes.

In the alternative method the eggs and potatoes tend to remain separate rather than integrated as shown above. Chop *3 medium to large potatoes coarsely,* parboil with *a teaspoon of salt* and leave to drain. Meanwhile, chop *a small to medium sized onion* and saute in *3 tablespoons of vegetable oil.* Stir fry $\frac{1}{2}$ *teaspoon of turmeric,* add the potatoes and mix thoroughly. Add *1 cup of cold water,* cover and leave to cook over a medium flame for about 10 minutes or until the potatoes are cooked. Add *4 eggs (size 2) and an additional* $\frac{3}{4}$ *teaspoon of salt.* Scramble, cover and simmer for 10 or 15 minutes. A handful of *fresh parsley or coriander leaves* may be chopped fine and sprinkled over the Mahmoosa. Alternatively *half a cupful of fresh tender celery stalks* may be used as a garnish.

Serve hot or cold with a slice of fresh lemon and chopped fresh chillies (optional).

Omelette

I don't wish merely to add one more variety to the innumerable varieties of omelettes, but here is one with a difference. For each person -

Prepare the mixture by separating *2 eggs.* Cream the yolks with *1 dessertspoon of finely chopped spring onions, 1 dessertspoon of finely chopped fresh coriander leaves, $\frac{1}{2}$ teaspoon of salt and pepper to taste.*

Whip the egg whites until stiff and firm. Fold the yolk mixture into the egg whites with a metal spoon.

Heat *2 tablespoons of vegetable or sunflower oil* in a shallow frying pan (6") and pour in the mixture over a medium to hot flame. When golden and crisp on one side, roll (like a Swiss roll) with a fork at one end and a palette knife at the other, in the frying pan

This should produce a golden brown casing with a soft centre. Serve hot.

Other leaves may be substituted for coriander, such as parsley or mint. Those who enjoy chillies can add them, chopped fine, into the yolk mixture.

Ujja

This is a cheese omelette but of a different variety to the above.

Grate *2 $\frac{1}{2}$ ozs of hard cheese* (Gouda for example) and blend with *1 large slightly whipped egg.* Add *a pinch of salt and pepper to taste.* Heat *2 tablespoons of vegetable or sunflower oil* in a shallow frying pan. (6"). Pour the mixture to cover the bottom of the pan. When golden brown on one side turn over and cook on the other until this side too is golden brown. Cook over a medium flame.

Serve hot with bread rolls.

Cheese ujja may also be eaten cold and makes a filling picnic food or packed lunch

Egg Mahmoosa

Egg mahmoosa is another version of the many varieties of shakshooka found throughout the Middle East. Suggested quantities for each person are -

Heat *2 dessertspoons of vegetable oil* in a small frying pan over medium heat. Saute *1 dessertspoon of finely chopped spring onions and chopped green chillies* (optional). Then add *2 chopped tomatoes,* simmer and stir occasionally until the mixture is pureed. Add *2 eggs, 1 dessertspoon of finely chopped coriander leaves, $\frac{1}{2}$ teaspoon salt and pepper to taste.*

Stir briskly until the mixture is just moist.

Serve hot.

Egg mahmoosa can be eaten with a variety of Indian or other bread.

Vegetable Cutlis

Vegetable cutlis makes a nutritious light meal or appetising starter served with a relish.

Boil *3 medium sized potatoes* in their jackets and *1 large carrot.* Parboil *2 ozs peas and 2 ozs sliced beans (any green variety will do).* If frozen vegetables are to be used immerse them in boiling water for 5 minutes. Mash the vegetables and add *1 heaped dessertspoon of finely chopped spring onions and 1 heaped dessertspoon of chopped green, yellow or red peppers.* These two ingredients provide the aromatic flavours. Add *a dessertspoon of freshly chopped coriander leaves (parsley or any other green herb).* Beat *an egg* lighly and add to the mixture together with *2 tablespoons of matzo meal (or breadcrumbs).* Add *1 $\frac{1}{2}$ teaspoons salt and pepper to taste.* Blend all the ingredients thoroughly.

Divide the mixture into 12 equal portions. Make into balls, flatten (but not too thin) crumb and deep fry over a medium to hot flame. Drain and serve hot.

All the preparation may be done in advance, leaving the frying for the last few minutes before serving.

Vegetable Patties

For the filling : Saute *1 medium sized onion* finely sliced. Any variety of vegetable may be combined and added - cauliflower florettes, mushrooms, peas, celery, beans potatoes, carrots, spinach, etc. Here is an example. Add *3 ozs fresh or frozen peas, 3 oz corn, 3 ozs sliced green beans, 2 medium sized chopped carrots, 3 medium size chopped potatoes.* Mix throughly, cover with cold water, boil and then simmer fo 20 - 30 minutes, or until the vegetables are tender but crisp. Add *3 teaspoon cumin powder, 4 teaspoons coriander powder, a large pinch of chillie powder - or mor (optional), 1 teaspoon salt and pepper to taste.* Simmer for another 5 minutes and add *th juice of half a lemon.* Cool.

Use puff pastry for the patties.

Assemble the patties : Divide the filling into 12 equal portions. Roll out the pastry enough for one pattie at a time, on a well floured board. Roll the pastry, the thickness o a pound piece, into squares. The pastry should not be rolled too thin or this will defeat th purpose of producing the layers in puff pastry, nor should it be too thick as this will detrac from the flavour of the filling. Make 4" squares for an entree dish or a picnic snack, 3 squares to serve with drinks. The aim is to get a triangle shape, so that the filling shoul be placed on one side of the square. The pastry should be folded down to cover the fillin; and the edges sealed with a little *lightly beaten egg.* Place on a baking sheet and glaze th top with beaten egg.

Bake in a preheated oven on the top shelf 400° Reg 6 for 15 - 20 minutes until golder brown.

The filling may be varied, either with a range of vegetables, egg and vegetables o poultry and vegetables.

Patties are best served hot. They can be cooked in advance and reheated for a fev minutes in a hot oven. Cold, they make an excellent picnic food or add variety to a buffe table.

Aloo Charp

"Aloo" is the Hindi word for potato. Aloo charp is egg shaped and is generally the size of a large egg. Aloo charp consists of a centre, which comes in a variety of fillings, encased in a thin coating of boiled potato which is then dipped in lightly beaten egg, covered with breadcrumbs, flour or matzo meal, and deep fried. To add variety, a little coriander powder and cumin powder may be added to the potato. This suggestion came from one of my daughters and it is this flexibility which makes cooking so enjoyable. Aloo charp served in Indian restaurants is altogether a different dish. Daisy Iny describes a dish from Baghdad called 'Urug' which is similar in all but detail to what is called Aloo charp here.

Egg aloo charp : Wash and boil *potatoes* in their jackets. For *each egg* boil *one potato* of roughly equivalent size. Peel and mash the potatoes until smooth. And *salt and pepper to taste*. Set aside.

Boil *eggs as required,* cut them in half, sprinkle with *salt, pepper* and a *generous squeeze of lemon juice* into the egg yolks.

Take the equivalent of half a boiled potato and flatten in the palm of your hand. Place an egg over it and wrap the potato around it until it is completely covered. Mould the potato around the egg to take its shape. Dip into a *lightly beaten egg* until each aloo charp is thoroughly covered, crumb and deep fry over a moderate to high flame until golden brown. Handle as little as possible while frying so that the potato casing does not break. Turn out and drain.

Serve hot or cold as required.

Vegetable aloo charp : This is made in the same way basically, except that the egg centre is substituted for a mixture of any chosen vegetables which can be boiled, or even better, taken from a prepared bhaji of your choice.

Chicken or meat aloo charp : Prepare the centre by frying *a small chopped onion.* When it is golden - brown cool and then add the required quantity of *minced chicken, beef or lamb.* Allow one tablespoon for each aloo charp. Add *salt and pepper* to taste and fry for half an hour or until the chicken or meat is cooked through. Break up with a fork from time to time during cooking. It is this filling, in particular, which is described in Baghdad cooking. The others would appear to have been developed in India. The centre may also be filled with chicken or meat which has already been cooked for a previous meal.

Aloo charp would make an excellent entree dish. The preparation can be done in advance, leaving the frying until the last few minutes before serving. However, it is also tasty served cold with a range of fresh salads.

Aubergine Cutlis

Saute *a medium sized onion* finely sliced in *2 tablespoons of vegetable oil*
When cool, add *1 lb of minced chicken, beef or lamb, ½ teaspoon of turmeric powder*
1 teaspoon of salt and pepper to taste. Mix thoroughly and cook on a low heat for half
an hour, turning the mince from time to time.

Meanwhile wash *3 medium sized aubergines.* Remove the stalks and cut the
aubergine in half lengthways. Remove the flesh so that a case remains which is of the
thickness of a pound coin and parboil. Chop the aubergine flesh finely, add to the cooked
mince and simmer for another five minutes.

Cool the mixture slightly and add *1 lightly beaten egg, 1 tablespoon of*
breadcrumbs or matzo meal and 1 tablespoon of chopped parsley or coriander leaves.

Fill the aubergine cases with this mixture, sprinkle the top with a light coating of
breadcrumbs or matzo meal and bake on a greased tray on the middle shelf of a preheated
oven gas mark 4, (350°F) for half an hour, or until the breadcrumbs are golden brown.
Serve hot.

One aubergine cutlis, garnished with a relish, provides an appetising starter.

Chicken Cutlis

Although chicken is used for this dish traditionally, slices of turkey breast or veal
would be equally suitable.

Three slices can be cut from each *breast of chicken* taken from a 5 lb roaster. This
should be a sufficient portion for each person served as a main meal with salads or cooked
vegetables. One or two slices should be enough for an entree dish served with a relish or
a slice of fresh lemon. This is excellent picnic food as it is just as delicious cold or hot

To prepare the egg mixture for *10 cutlis* - Beat *1 egg* lightly. Add *1 grated onion*
(medium sized), 2 teaspoons grated ginger, 1 teaspoon grated garlic, ½ teaspoon
turmeric powder, 1 teaspoon salt and pepper to taste. Beat together so that the
ingredients are thoroughly mixed.

Slightly salt each cutlis, score the chicken and dip into the egg mixture, covering
it thoroughly and making sure that some of the onion, garlic and ginger adhere. Coat each
cutlis with matzo meal or breadcrumbs and deep fry.

Chicken Rissoles

This is a favourite with children in particular and is a convenient picnic food. erved hot with a variety of salads and sometimes with chappatis or pitta bread it will do s a main meal, but a couple on their own or with a relish would be suitable as an entree ish.

Mince *2 lbs of chicken breasts* (minced veal or turkey would also be delicious) and dd *1 medium sized onion* chopped fine, *1 dessertspoon grated ginger,* $\frac{1}{2}$ *dessertspoon rated garlic (optional) 1 teaspoon turmeric powder, 1 teaspoon salt, pepper to taste, beaten egg and 2 tablespoons matzo meal or breadcrumbs.*

For variety, I sometimes add *1 teaspoon onion seeds or 1 dessertspoon chopped arsley or coriander leaves.*

Mix all the ingredients together until it has the consistency of a firm dough. If it is ioist add more matzo meal.

In a deep frying pan, bring *vegetable or sunflower oil* to the boil. Meanwhile spread iatzo meal crumbs on a board. Take enough mixture, about the size of a walnut, make into a ball, flatten it (but not too thin) on the bed of crumbs and fry. Drain.

The above quantity should produce sixteen rissoles.

Kebab

The uniqueness of a kebab depends upon the marinade. Grilled over an open fire chicken, fish or meat is delicious. For indoor cooking a very hot grill is best but for large quantities the top shelf of a hot oven gas mark 7 produces good results.

Kebab may be served as an entree dish, in which case a quarter pound of chicken breasts and wings, white fish, or lamb per person should be sufficient. For a main course allow half a pound per person. Any variety of fresh salads would go well with kebab as a starter; for a main course pilaw or allomakalla may be added.

To make the marinade, pour *3 tablespoons of vegetable oil* into a large bowl. Add the *juice of half a lemon, $\frac{1}{2}$ teaspoon of salt and pepper to taste, $\frac{1}{2}$ teaspoon turmeric, 1 small grated onion, 2 teaspoons grated ginger and 1 teaspoon crushed garlic (optional) and 1 teaspoon of onion seeds.* The onion seeds give the marinade its unique flavour and are widely available in Indian grocery or greengrocery shops. The Indian word for onion seeds is KOOLONJI.

2lbs of chicken, white fish, or lamb should be cut into mouth-sized pieces, washed, dried and put into the marinade. Mix all the ingredients thoroughly and allow to stand covered in the refrigerator for at least 2 hours.

When ready to cook, the pieces may be skewered or laid flat on foil over the rack of the grill pan. The kebabs should be watched carefully while cooking to make sure the pieces do not burn or dry out as they should remain moist and succulent. When one side has been cooked, turn the kebabs over.

Serve hot.

Hussaine Kebab

Cut *1 lb of shoulder of lamb* or *2 large chicken breasts* into mouth-sized pieces. Marinade in *2 tablespoons of vegetable oil, the juice of 1 lemon, 1 dessertspoon cumin powder, 1 dessertspoon coriander powder, $\frac{1}{2}$ teaspoon turmeric, $\frac{1}{2}$ teaspoon salt and pepper to taste, 1 small grated onion, 1 teaspoon grated garlic.* Cover and allow to rest in the refrigerator for at least 2 hours.

In India, the Moslem community usually marinade chicken and meat in youghurt in preparation for kebabs. This tenderises the meat. Since this method would not be acceptable in Jewish cooking, the youghurt may be substituted by 2 teaspoons of mayonnaise.

Slice very fine *1 oz of fresh root ginger.* Thread this alternately with the lamb or chicken breasts on skewers and grill or barbecue until cooked through.

Serve hot with salads and pitta bread or chappatis.

Hussaine Kebab will add variety to a barbecue party or provide an appetising first course at a dinner party.

Masala Kebab

This is a spiced kebab, more appropriate for lamb or chicken than fish. For *1lb of shoulder of lamb* or *2 large chicken breasts* cut into mouth-sized pieces, use the following marianade.

1 large grated onion, 4 cloves of grated garlic, 1 teaspoon grated fresh ginger, to which should be added *1 dessertspoon cumin powder, 1 dessertspoon coriander powder, $\frac{1}{2}$ teaspoon turmeric, 1 teaspoon powdered cinnamon, 1 teaspoon alspice, 4 cloves and 4 crushed cardimum pods, $\frac{1}{2}$ teaspoon ground red chillies* (optional). Pour in the juice of *half a lemon* and *3 tablespoons of vegetable oil.* Mix throughly with the addition of *3 tablespoons tomato puree,* and *2 teaspoons of mayonnaise.*

Cover and allow to rest in the refrigerator for at least two hours - preferably longer.

Either skewer the pieces or lay flat on foil over the rack of a grill pan. Cook under hot grill, ensuring that the pieces of meat or chicken do not dry out or overcook. Turn from time to time.

Serve hot.

Koorket

Koorket is a sausage-shaped rissole made with minced chicken, lamb or beef.

Chop a *medium sized onion* and fry in *2 tablespoons of vegetable oil*. When golde brown, cool, and add *1 lb of minced chicken, beef or lamb (after the fat has bee trimmed),* $\frac{1}{2}$ *teaspoon of* turmeric powder, $\frac{1}{2}$ *teaspoon salt and pepper to taste, an 2 slices of bread softened in water and with the crusts trimmed.* Mix thoroughly an cook for half an hour, stirring from time to time on a low heat. When the chicken c meat is cooked, cool the mixture and beat in *1 egg* and enough *matzo meal o breadcrumbs* to make a dough-like consistency.

Wet your hands, take a small quantity of the mixture, about the size of a walnu shape into a ball and then roll into a sausage shape - about $3\frac{1}{2}$ inches long. When all th koorkets have been prepared in this way, crumb and deep fry until golden brown. Ca should be taken not to move them while deep frying so that they don't break.

Drain and serve hot with a relish.

Mahasha

Mahashas are stuffed vegetables. This is a common dish throughout the Middle East, the variations being in the selection of vegetables and the ingredients used for stuffing them. A wide range of vegetables or leaves may be stuffed and cooked in one saucepan without ruining the flavour of any particular vegetable. Tomatoes, yellow, green and red peppers, small aubergines (from India), and small cucumbers (from Cyprus or India) are all suitable. The vegetables are prepared by slicing the top three-quarters of the way through to make a lid, and scooping out the flesh which can be combined to prepare a separate delicious vegetable dish in an onion sauce. Onion skins are prepared by peeling one or two medium to large sized onions, slitting them halfway through one side, and parboiling until the layers are tender enough to be separated from each other. Each layer forms a separate case and about four cases may be had from a single onion. Lettuce or vine leaves (from Cyprus) should be blanched and the centre beaten to soften.

For stuffing a mixture of 4 medium sized tomatoes, 5 onion skins, 4 small cucumbers and 3 small peppers,

Wash & parboil $\frac{1}{2}$ *lb white rice*. Alternatively the rice can be left standing in boiling water for 20 minutes. Basmati or Patna rice would both be suitable but Patna has the slight edge as it cooks through very quickly.

Add the following ingredients to the rice -
2 small breasts of chicken cut in small cubes or minced coarsely
$\frac{1}{2}$ teaspoon of fresh ginger grated or finely chopped
$\frac{1}{2}$ teaspoon fresh garlic grated or crushed
2 tablespoons of finely chopped mint or tender celery leaves
2 teaspoons sugar
$\frac{1}{2}$ teaspoon turmeric powder
Juice of 1 lemon
1 tablespoon oil
2 teaspoons salt
Pepper to taste

For a purely vegetarian stuffing the chicken can be left out and the rice increased to produce the required bulk.

Fill each vegetable three-quarters of the way to the top or when filling the onion skins or leaves make sure there is room for the rice to swell when cooking.

Grease the bottom of a heavy, wide based saucepan and place the stuffed vegetables, leaves and onion skins side by side. Sprinkle the tops with *a shake of salt, pepper, turmeric, sugar and lemon juice* to flavour the casings. Cover and bake in a preheated oven on the middle shelf (350°F Reg.4) for half an hour. Uncover and cook for another half an hour ensuring the rice has cooked through before serving.

As an entree dish perhaps one or two varieties may be prepared and an onion and tomato mahasha, for example would provide an excellent starter to a meal. However, a variety of stuffed vegetables, each providing its own particular flavour could make a main meal served with a relish and a variety of salads.

Although mahashas are best served hot, they are also delicious at room temperature and lend both colour and interest to a buffet table.

Pantras

Pantras is a filled pancake which is then deep fried. The filling is usually made with minced chicken or meat but there is no reason why cheese or vegetable fillings may not be used instead. I shall concentrate here on the traditional chicken or meat filling.

Start by preparing the filling : Saute *a medium sized onion* finely sliced in *2 tablespoons of vegetable oil.* Cool the onions slightly and add *1 lb of minced chicken, beef or lamb,* $\frac{1}{2}$ *teaspoon of turmeric powder,* $\frac{1}{2}$ *teaspoon of salt and pepper* to taste and *1 tablespoon of chopped fresh coriander or parsley leaves.* Mix thoroughly and cook over low heat for half an hour, turning from time to time.

A larger quantity of this filling may be cooked in advance and stored in a few small containers in the freezer, to be used as required for a number of dishes, such as koorke aubengine cutlis and chicken sumoosucks.

Meanwhile mix *1 cup of plain flour with 1 small egg,* $\frac{1}{2}$ *teaspoon of salt and 1* $\frac{1}{4}$ *cups of cold water.* Allow the mixture to stand for half an hour.

To make the pancakes : Grease the bottom of a 6" frying pan and place over a high flame. Then reduce the heat and place about two tablespoons of the mixture in the pan roll the mixture around until it spreads around the bottom of the pan. As soon as the edge have cooked the pancake can be flipped out and the uncooked side placed on a crumbe board.

Fill the pancake (ie the cooked side) with a tablespoon of the *cooled* filling. Roll into a cigar shape, tucking in the top and bottom, and sealing, if necessary, with a few drops of the pancake mixture.

When the filled pancakes have been prepared, deep fry until golden-brown and serve hot with a relish.

This is the traditional way to prepare pantras which is usually eaten as an entree dish but it can also be made in a large frying pan and served as a main course with a variety of fillings such as vegetables and cold sliced chicken with a few flakes of skinned citrus fruit such as orange and grapefruit.

Shoofta

Shoofta is a versatile dish - it is possible to use minced chicken, fish or veal as a base, with equally good results. As with other light dishes, shoofta can be enjoyed with any dish with a number of fresh salads, or with cooked vegetables.

Traditionally shooftas are cooked on skewers over an open coal fire but they can also be grilled, baked or fried. Quantities here are for 12 shooftas.

GRILLED

Mince *1 lb of chicken breast, veal, or white fish* . Chop *1 dessertspoon of fresh ginger* and *1 dessertspoon of fresh garlic very fine* and add to the minced chicken, veal or fish. Add *1 medium sized onion* chopped very fine, $\frac{1}{2}$ *teaspoon turmeric, 1 teaspoon salt, pepper to taste and 1 tablespoon of finely chopped tender celery leaves or fresh mint.* Other green herbs may be substituted, for example, basil or majoram would be very suitable. Add *1 tablespoon of vegetable, corn or sunflower oil* to the mixture and mix into a soft dough-like consistency. With wet hands, divide the mixture into 12 equal portions. Each portion should be made into a sausage shape, and placed on a sheet of aluminium foil and grilled on a high flame, first on one side and then on the other, until golden brown.

For grilling over charcoal, take each portion and work around a skewer, aiming at sausage shape. More than one shoofta can be made around a large skewer
Serve on a warm dish and garnish with the same leaf used in the mixture.

BAKED

Make each portion into a sausage shape and place on a baking tray. Bake in a preheated oven on the top shelf on 440° Reg. or gas mark 8, for 10 minutes until the shooftas are brown.

FRIED

An equally delicious result may be obtained by covering the bottom of a frying pan generously with *vegetable oil.* Bring to the boil and turn down to cook on a very low light, easing each shoofta into the pan. When one side becomes firm (not brown), turn. Cover the frying pan when both sides are firm and turn up to medium heat. Cook for 5 minutes or until one side is golden brown. Turn and brown the other side. Add enough *cold water* very carefully until all the shooftas are covered. Bring to the boil, cover and cook for 10 minutes. Remove the cover and cook for 5 minutes more.

Serve on a warm dish and garnish.

Shooftas are best when served hot but they are perfectly acceptable as a cold meal and picnic food.

Chicken Summoosucks

Soak **4 oz chick peas** overnight. Boil the following day until the chick peas are soft enough to mash with a fork.

Saute a **small onion** chopped fine. When it is cool add **4 oz minced breast of chicken, veal or beef**. When the mince is golden brown add the mashed chick peas and season with **1 tablespoon cumin powder, 1½ tablespoons coriander powder, the juice of half a lemon, chillie powder, salt and pepper** to taste.

Traditionally the filling is placed in a pastry case made with **6 oz self raising flour, 3 ozs margarine, ½ teaspoon salt** with enough water to make a firm but soft dough and deep fried. Puff pastry is a very acceptable alternative. Roll out the pastry into 3" or 4" squares as required.

Place a spoonful of filling on one side of the square, turning down the other side. Seal the edges with a drop of water. Bake in a hot pre-heated oven, gas mark 6 for 15 to 20 minutes or until the pastry is golden brown. The top of the pastry may be brushed with egg yolk to improve browning.

This was a popular party food and was eaten on the Festival of Simhat Torah in some homes, not as a symbolic food in religious terms but as a food associated with good times.

Fish Aruktaheen

Fish aruktaheen is an excellent starter or makes a delicious snack with drinks.
Combine $\frac{3}{4}$ *lb of minced fish* (white fish is most suitable) or fish roe with *1 medium sized onion chopped fine, 1 teaspoon fresh ginger, 1 crushed clove of garlic, tablespoon coriander leaves* (this may be substituted by other fresh green herbs such s marjoram, parsley, basil), $\frac{1}{2}$ *cup plain flour, $\frac{1}{2}$ teaspoon turmeric, $\frac{1}{2}$ teaspoon salt nd pepper to taste, 1 chopped green chillie (optional).*
This should be made into a dough-like consistency, divided into 12 equal portions, made into balls with wet hands, flattened and deep fried over medium heat.
Serve hot.

Plain Aruktaheen

This is a vegetarian version and is made in the above way, but without the fish. The consistency should nevertheless resemble dough, that is the ingredients should hold together to make a number of distinctive balls.

Fish Cutlis

Remove the crust from *2 slices of white bread* and soak in water for a couple of minutes. Squeeze out the water and crumble the bread into *1 lb of flaked white fish.* Add *small chopped onion, 1 tablespoon tomato sauce, 1 teaspoon salt and pepper to taste.* One tablespoon of chopped coriander leaves or parsley is optional.
Divide the mixture into balls the size of a walnut. Flatten, *coat with breadcrumbs or matzo meal* and deep fry in hot oil.
Drain and serve hot with a variety of vegetables and relishes.

Rice Dishes

Early training in picking rice to remove the husks and grit.
Dietary laws require all food to be prepared with care.

Rice Dishes

Rice is a staple grain in India but it is also very popular in the Middle East. A range f pilaw dishes form an important part of the cooking of Northern Indian and it is quite kely that the Moghul Emperors who arrived on the Indian scene from Persia brought 1ese culinery delights with them. In this way the Muslims of India were the carriers of 1any Middle Eastern dishes. The Jews who migrated to India from Iraq and Syria :inforced this process to some extent.

Some of the rice dishes here are eaten together with other foods to provide a main 1eal; others are main meals cooked with chicken or fish. The rice dishes here straddle oth light and substantial dishes.

Humeen

Most Jewish communities have devised a dish to cook very slowly overnight on th
Sabbath to provide a hot meal without violating the Sabbath laws which prohibit work o
that day. Humeen - sometimes pronounced slightly differently in other communities i
the Middle East - appears to be the generic name given to the hot meal served on th
Sabbath. It is usually rice-based but differs regionally.

There is, of course, no reason why Humeen should necessarily be served only o
the Sabbath or why it should only be cooked overnight. Alternative methods will b
suggested here. This is a delicious dish, very easy to prepare, and may be served with
range of relishes or with a fresh green salad.

Saute a medium-sized sliced *onion.* Wash, and add *2 cups of white rice, salt d
pepper,* $\frac{1}{2}$ *teaspoon turmeric, 4 cloves, 4 cardimum pods and a large stick of cinnamon
(A bay leaf is optional).* Fry for a couple of minutes. Add *1 teaspoon grated fresh ginge*
(or 1 teaspoon ginger powder) *and two grated cloves of garlic* (also optional). Add th
pieces of a *5 lb roasting chicken together with 1 oz of chicken fat* ; this is important a
it stops the Humeen from being dry and stir fry until all the ingredients are mixe
thoroughly. Add *1 cup of cold water,* turn on to a hot flame until the water is absorbe
stirring from time to time. Add *1 more cup of cold water,* cover, bring to the boil and bak
on the middle shelf of the oven on gas mark 5 for 1 hour. Remove from the oven, stir an
return to the oven for another half an hour or until the chicken is tender and the rice cooke
through. If necessary, add a little more water at this stage.

This is the traditional way to cook a basic Humeen. The taste alters ver
considerably if tomatoes are added. If this is preferred, the *tomatoes, fresh or tinned,* ma
be put in once the onions are sauted. *8 ounces* should be sufficient for a 5 lb roastin
chicken. Alternatively, 2 ounces of pureed tomato may be used.

On special occasions, dried fruit, such as apricots would be added instead c
tomatoes, and when in season, pieces of fresh quince. It is also possible to substitute ric
with barley. Another variation is carrot humeen. Add *1 lb of whole carrots,* or cut int
strips, with the chicken pieces.

The method shown above is the traditonal way to cook Humeen. If time is at
premium, why not try a shorter way which I have used quite successfully ? Place all th
ingredients in the saucepan at one time, don't saute the onion simply slice it fine or cho
it. Mix everything thoroughly and bake as shown above.

If Humeen is to be prepared for the Sabbath it must be placed in the oven just befo
Sabbath comes in. It should be cooked on gas mark $\frac{1}{2}$, or a very low light until lunch tim
on Saturday. When cooked very slowly it is not necessary to remove it and stir half wa
through the cooking. It is advisable to use a heavy saucepan.

It was customary, in many homes, to roast a few eggs for the sabbath by placin
them on the inverted saucepan lid of the dish of Humeen.

Hushwa

Traditionally Hushwa is stuffing in the skin of a chicken. Skinning is time consuming for those who haven't acquired the skill. Alternatively, it is easier to stuff a chicken, or any other bird, while it is roasting whole and this is quite successful using the traditional ingredients. Hushwa in skin was cooked in the same saucepan as humeen or turikebab or in a pan by itself. If a *chicken is to be skinned,* start at the rump and proceed towards the neck of the bird.

Wash *1 cup of white rice* and cover with *1 cup of boiling water.* Cook for a quarter of an hour on the boil. Drain in cold water and add *1 tablespoon of vegetable oil* or 1 oz of chicken fat, $\frac{1}{4}$ *teaspoon of turmeric powder, 2 cloves, 2 pods of cardimum,* $\frac{1}{2}$ *teaspoon of ginger powder* (or $\frac{1}{2}$ teaspoon of fresh grated ginger), *2 cloves of grated garlic is optional, 1 teaspoon of salt and pepper to taste.* Slice or chop the *gizzard of the chicken,* making sure the gristle is discarded, and add to the mixture.

Mix all the ingredients thoroughly, stuff the chicken and roast. Or, stuff the skin of the chicken, but not too tightly, sew and roast in a greased saucepan for 45 minutes or until the skin is crisp and brown. Roast on gas mark 6, middle shelf, in a preheated oven, and baste from time to time.

This stuffing can be served with roast poultry or meat, and if cooked with humeen, can be served together with it.

Khitchree

Although this dish may be thought to be typically Indian as it is made with rice and lentils, both staple grains in that country, reference to Daisy Iny's book suggests that it was in the repertoire from Baghdad. This is probably one example of a dish which was introduced from the Middle East to India during the period of the Moghul Empire, or it could have been introduced to the Middle East by traders from India.

Fry together *1 cup of white rice,* $\frac{1}{2}$ *cup of red lentils ("Dal"), 1* $\frac{1}{2}$ *teaspoons of cumin powder, 3 cloves of garlic chopped fine,* $\frac{1}{2}$ *teaspoon of turmeric powder in 3 tablespoons of oil.* Stir for about five minutes over moderate heat until the ingredients combine and the aroma of the cumin and garlic rises.

Add *1* $\frac{1}{2}$ *cups of boiling water,* bring this to the boil, cover and then bake on a low light - gas mark 1 or 150° for 20 minutes. Turn the rice mixture with a spatula and bake for another 20 minutes.

Khitchree is a delicious rice dish and may be eaten with a bhaji, with a salad or with relishes. This dish is nutritious and would suit vegetarians especially well.

Pilaw

Pilaws or pilaffs, as this rice-based dish is known in some parts of the world, ar made in different ways in different regions. A plain pilaw makes a pleasant change fror boiled rice and this is the traditional way to prepare it.

Wash the required quantity; 2 ozs is usually sufficient for one portion. White ric only should be used. Patna and Basmati are both very suitable varieties. For *1 cup of ric* add *1 tablespoon of vegetable or corn oil, $\frac{1}{4}$ teaspoon of turmeric powder, 3 cloves, . cardimum pods, a large stick of cinnamon and 1 teaspoon of salt. A bay leaf* is optiona

Stir fry for a couple of minutes to ensure all the ingredients are thoroughly mixe

Cover with *1 cup of boiling water* and bring to the boil. Cover and place on th middle shelf of a preheated oven on gas mark 2 for 20 minutes.

If you are cooking in a non-stick pan, leave until the cooking is complete Otherwise, remove from the oven after 15 minutes. Make sure the rice does not cling t the sides of the pan by heaping it towards the middle. Return to the oven for a further . minutes to complete the cooking.

Serve hot with a variety of dishes as suggested elsewhere.

On festival days or on private celebrations such as weddings and birthdays, pila was always served with a generous sprinkling of almonds and raisins on the the top Cookery books from the Middle East indicate that this is common practice in the entir region. The raisins should be washed and dried. The almonds blanched and slivered. Fr the almonds first until golden; remove from the pan and fry the raisins in the same oil unt they plump up. Drain and sprinkle on the pilaw.

Pilaw Matabakh

This is a fish and vegetable pilaw which looks very colourful. It is best served hot but would be suitable for a cold table.

Prepare the pilaw by washing *2 cups of rice.* Stir fry for a couple of minutes in *3 tablespoons of vegetable or corn oil.* Add *3 cloves, 3 cardimum pods, $\frac{1}{2}$ teaspoon turmeric powder, a large stick of cinnamon and 1 teaspoon of salt.* Add enough *cold water* to just cover the rice. Bring to the boil and simmer until the water has evaporated. Set aside. The rice should be partially cooked.

Meanwhile slice *3 large onions into rings* and saute. Set aside and drain.

Fry *3 lbs of white fish* (haddock or cod would be suitable) filletted and cut into individual portions with the skin on so that the fish does not break up. To prepare the fish, wash, dry and *sprinkle lightly with salt and turmeric powder* and lower straight into *hot oil* (no batter or crumbing is necessary.) Set aside on absorbent paper and remove the skin. The fish should be fried until it just turns golden.

Remove the skin and pith of a large lemon and cut into fine slices.

Set aside. Lemboo Basra is however the authentic traditional ingredient.

Pick over an ounce of coriander leaves from the stalks, wash, dry and set aside.

Continue by using a fireproof dish which can be brought from the oven to the table. This dish should have a wide base so that layers of the above ingredients may be built up. Smear the bottom of the dish generously with *vegetable oil.* Cover with a layer of half the onions, a layer of half the fish portions, a layer of lemon slices - dotted around rather than side by side - half the partially cooked pilaw, topped with half the fresh coriander leaves. Build the layers again from the onions up to the coriander leaves, using all the remaining ingredients. Add $\frac{3}{4}$ *cup of warm water* and bake, covered, in a preheated oven, on the middle shelf, gas mark 2 for 20 minutes, by which time the water should have been absorbed and the rice cooked through.

Serve with a large spatula, reaching down to the bottom of the dish, trying to preserve the layers as they were cooked.

Serve with a chopped fresh vegetable salad using, for example, tomatoes, cucumber, celery stalks, white cabbage, and carrots.

Vegetable Pilaw

Vegetable pilaws are well known both in the Middle East and in India. The metho of preparation and the taste varies almost from home to home. The way suggested her has Middle Eastern elements which were developed in India.

Slice *a medium sized onion* as finely as possible and saute in *3 tablespoons o vegetable or corn oil.* Make sure the onions are glazed and not golden brown, becaus they should remain soft rather than crisp. Add *8 ozs of chopped fresh or canned tomatoe:* Stir and reduce to make a sauce. Wash and add *1 cup of white rice, 2 ozs peas, and 2 oz of chopped beans.* Additional vegetables may be added such as diced carrots, smal cauliflower florettes and chopped potatoes. Sprinkle with *1 teaspoon of salt,* $\frac{1}{4}$*teaspoo of turmeric powder,* and add *3 cloves, 3 cardimum pods and 1 large stick of cinnamon* Stir fry for a minute or two until all the ingredients are thoroughly mixed.

Cover with *1 cup of boiling water* and bring to the boil. Cover the saucepan an place in a preheated oven on gas mark 2 for 20 minutes. If a non-stick pan is used, leav in the oven until the cooking is complete. Otherwise remove after 15 minutes, make sur the rice does not cling to the sides by making a mound in the middle, return to the ove for another 5 minutes and the pilaw is ready to serve.

Serve with a range of dishes such as curries, khuttas and bhajis.

Main Meals

"Poultry, poultry, poultry for a bargain, Sir"

Main Meals

The dishes here would be suitable for a main course or provide a complete meal rved with rice, potatoes, fresh or cooked vegetables as suggested in each case.

These dishes are mainly dry, or curried in a little sauce. The curries are modified dian recipes and suggestions will be made for preparing them either mild or strong. ne quantities suggested in this section are aimed at serving 4 to 6 portions.

Bamboo Curry

Curried dishes are derived from Indian cooking but to conform to dietary laws wish communities have had to make certain modifications. For example, oil is ibstituted for butter and curries cooked in yoghurt or cream sauces may sametimes be ombined with fish, but not with meat or poultry. For this reason, cream of coconut milk sometimes used or dairy produce is omitted altogether.

Bamboo in brine is available in most Indian grocery shops. An *8 oz tin* should e used with a *4 $\frac{1}{2}$ lb chicken or 2 $\frac{1}{2}$ lbs of white fish.*

Drain the bamboo, wash and parboil. Chop the bamboo and set aside.

For a chicken meal, joint the chicken, wash and set aside.

Saute *a medium sized onion,* then add $\frac{1}{2}$ *teaspoon turmeric, salt and pepper to iste, 3 teaspoons cumin powder, 5 teaspoons coriander powder, 4 large cloves of grated arlic, 1 teaspoon grated ginger, 1 teaspoon chillie powder (optional).*

Blend the ingredients thoroughly, stir frying for a few minutes, add *1 cup of water* nd the jointed chicken. Stir fry until the spices coat the chicken pieces. Add the bamboo. 1elt an *8 oz bar of cream of cocount* in *half a cup of boiling water.* When the bar has issolved, stir into the curry.

Cover, and bake in a preheated oven on gas mark 5, (550°) middle shelf for an hour nd a half, or until the chicken is tender.

Serve hot with rice or pilaw.

The chicken and bamboo may also be prepared without the curry spices.

Fish—particularly white varieties—may be substituted for chicken and again there ; the alternative of adding or deleting the curry spices. The cooking time will be half an our on gas mark 4 (450°).

Bombay Curry

This is an extremely hot curry and should be eaten with a very generous portion of boiled rice.

Fry *3 large onions* chopped fine in *4 tablespoons of vegetable oil o chicken fat.* When the onions are golden brown add *3 teaspoons of crushe ginger, 1 ½ teaspoons of crushed garlic, 12 whole fresh red chillies, 2 ½ teaspoons o coriander powder, 1 teaspoon of cumin powder, ½ teaspoon of turmeric, salt and peppe to taste.* Fry the spices with the onions until the aroma rises and add the pieces of a *4 roasting chicken.* Seal over a hot flame, cover and place on the middle shelf of moderately hot oven—gas mark 5—for an hour or until the chicken is tender.

Add *2 tablespoons of vinegar and 2 teaspoons of sugar.* Mix thoroughly, adju the seasoning and serve hot.

Chicken & Dal Curry

This is very much a hybrid dish—Middle Eastern origins with a distinct India influence.

Fry a *medium sized sliced onion* until golden brown. Add *½ teaspoon turmeri salt, pepper, 2 grated cloves of garlic (optional), 1 teaspoon grated fresh ginger o ginger powder, 1 green chillie slit down one side (optional).* Stir fry for a couple o minutes. Add the pieces of a *4-5 lb roasting chicken.* Stir fry the above mixture wit *1 cup of cold water.* Bring to the boil and reduce the water on a hot flame, stirring all th while. Set aside.

Meanwhile prepare the dal separately. Pick over *8 ozs of masoor dal* (the orang coloured variety), wash thoroughly, cover and boil in *1 pint of cold water* for half an hou by which time the dal should have broken down. Stir from time to time. Add *tw tablespoons of lukewarm water* as this will make the mixture smooth. Add salt to tast

Take *1 tablespoon of cumin powder, 1 teaspoon of garlic and pinch of turmeri* and fry in *2 tablespoons of hot oil* for a minute or two. Pour over the dal and mi thoroughly. Continue boiling uncovered until the dal is reduced to a thick paste.

Add the dal to the chicken pieces and bake in a moderate oven, gas mark 4, middl shelf, for an hour.

Serve hot with boiled rice or pilaw.

Chicken and Peas

Saute *1 medium sized onion in 3 tablespoons of vegetable oil.* When the onions e glazed add $\frac{1}{2}$ *teaspoon of turmeric, 2$\frac{1}{2}$ lbs of peas, salt and pepper to taste.* Some milies add *1 teaspoon of grated ginger and $\frac{1}{2}$ teaspoon of grated garlic* but this is tional. Stir fry until the ingredients are thoroughly mixed. Add the pieces of a *4$\frac{1}{2}$ lb asting chicken with $\frac{1}{2}$ pint of cold water.* Bring this to the boil and simmer until the ater is reduced. Add *2 tablespoons of chopped fresh coriander leaves* and mix oroughly.

Cover the saucepan and bake on gas mark 6, middle shelf, in a preheated oven for hour.

Adjust the seasoning and serve hot with rice, pilaw or potatoes.

Chiturney

This is a sweet-sour chicken curry and is generally eaten on a bed of boiled rice or law. Some people prefer to delete the curry powders so that the chicken is cooked in a veet-sour sauce only. It is, in fact, the way it used to be prepared in Baghdad. The ddition of curry powders is an Indian development.

Joint, clean and skin a *5lb roaster* and set aside.

Liquidise together, or chop very fine, *3 large onions, 4 large cloves of garlic, 1 oz esh ginger and $\frac{1}{2}$ lb fresh or canned tomatoes.*

Heat *3 tablespoons vegetable or corn oil,* add the liquidised mixture and cook over low heat until the onions are sauted. Add *2 teaspoons salt, pepper to taste, 1 teaspoon urmeric powder, and 4 tablespoons tomato puree.* Mix thoroughly.

Add the chicken pieces and seal on a high flame. Reduce to medium heat and cook ith the lid on for a quarter of an hour or until most of the juices are absorbed into the hicken. Add 1 *cup boiling water,* cover and simmer or bake on gas mark 4 (450°) until e chicken is tender (about half to three-quarters of an hour). Add *1 teaspoon chillie owder (or to taste), 4 teaspoons coriander powder (Dhunia), 3 teaspoons cumin owder (Zeera), 2 teaspoons sugar and the juice of 1$\frac{1}{2}$ to 2 lemons.* The balance etween the lemon juice and sugar depends on the extent to which the sweet-sour flavour ; preferred.

Tamarind paste may be substituted for lemon juice, in which case use 3 teaspoons, ut many people prefer vinegar (either the malt or wine variety, depending on the edge r smoothness preferred)

Stir for 5 minutes to blend all the flavours.

Serve hot with boiled rice or pilaw.

Curried Hussainie Kebab

Prepare the marinade as shown for Hussainie Kebab . Thread the meat or chicke slices with slivers of fresh root ginger on kebab sticks or small skewers. Set aside.

Grate or liquidise *2 large onions* and fry in *4 tablespoons of vegetable oil* unt golden-brown. *Add ½ pint of cold water and bring to the boil. Place the stick kebabs i this sauce with 2 cardimums and 2 cloves.* Simmer and reduce the liquid until the wate is nearly absorbed. *Sprinkle 2 teaspoons of coriander powder and 1 teaspoon of cumi powder,* adjust the salt and add *1 tablespoon of lemon juice* (optional).

Allow the kebabs to cook in the added ingredients for five minutes, shake the pa to ensure the kebabs are thoroughly mixed with the sauce and spices and serve hot wi rice, pilaw or aloomakala.

This dish was developed by one of the cooks in my aunt's household. The Hussaini Kebab, like most other kebabs, is probably of Middle Eastern origin. We owe it to th cooks in our household for much of the expansion in our cuisine and this was done largel by adapting to Indian styles of cooking.

Curried Lamb and Rice

The relatively high spicing of this dish suggests an Indian influence although ri and meat cooked together was not uncommon in the Baghdadi tradition.

Slice *1 lb of onions*—not too fine—and saute in *2 tablespoons of vegetable o* When the onions are glazed add *2 ½ lbs of lamb* trimmed and cut into mouth sized piece Seal the lamb with the onions over a high flame, making sure the meat has browned c all sides. Season the meat and onions with *1 stick of cinnamon, 2 cloves, 2 pods cardimum, 3 bay leaves, 2 teaspoons of coriander powder, 1 teaspoon of cumi powder, ½ teaspoon of turmeric powder, 3 grated cloves of garlic, 1 teaspoon of grate fresh ginger, and chillie powder to taste. Add ½ pint of cold water and bring this the boil with salt and pepper to taste.*

Cover the saucepan and place in a preheated oven on gas mark 6 for an hour or un the meat is tender. Keep warm on the lowest heat in the bottom of the oven.

In the meantime wash and drain 2 cups of white rice in a separate saucepan. Remo enough liquid from the meat so that the level is about half an inch above the rice.

Return the meat to a warm oven. Bring the rice to the boil and then place in the ov on gas mark 2 for a quarter of an hour. Add the lamb to the rice, mix thoroughly, ar continue to cook until the rice has completed cooking. If necessary add a little water the rice. Adjust the seasoning and serve hot with a selection of relishes.

Dopyasa

Dopyasa is chicken or lamb curry in a rich onion sauce. The Indian way to prepare is to add yoghurt or cream to the sauce but this is omitted from the repertoire of the wish community.

The recipe here is for Dopyasa cooked with either a $4\frac{1}{2}$ *lb jointed chicken, or, lb of chicken livers,* or *4 lbs of stewing lamb.*

Slice and saute *3 medium sized onions in 3 tablespoons of vegetable oil. Add heaped teaspoon of grated ginger, 1 heaped teaspoon of grated garlic, 1 teaspoon of rmeric, salt and pepper to taste, and 1 teaspoon of chillie powder (optional).* Stir fry ntil all the ingredients are blended. Add *1lb of potatoes* cut in cubes and *1 cup of water.* arboil.

Add the jointed chicken, chicken livers or stewing lamb and work into the sauce ntil it is slightly reduced on a high flame.

Add *5 teaspoons dhunia (coriander powder), 3 teaspoons zeera powder (cumin),* ix well, cover, and bake in a preheated oven on gas mark 5 (550°) for an hour (half an our for the liver).

Serve hot on a bed of rice or pilaw.

Chicken Hurikebab

This dish is a great favourite. I shall first outline the traditional way of preparir it which was suited to brick and clay fires and then an adapted method using oven cookin The ingredients for either method are the same.

Traditional cooking : Joint and skin a *5 lb roasting chicken*. Wash, and set asid Slice and saute *a small onion in 4 tablespoons of vegetable oil* or 3 ozs of chicken fa Add *1 teaspoon grated ginger, $\frac{1}{2}$ teaspoon turmeric, 1 teaspoon garlic (optional), teaspoons salt and pepper to taste, 3 cloves, 3 cardimum pods.* Stir-fry for 2 minute Add the chicken pieces, and stir until thoroughly blended with the spiced onions. Put tl lid on the saucepan and simmer for 15 minutes. When the juices have evaporated add tl required whole onions (small) and peeled but whole potatoes for five or six people. Tl contents of the saucepan should be alongside rather than on top of each other. Add ju enough water to cover the chicken pieces. Bring to the boil and simmer for $\frac{3}{4}$ of an hor with the lid on. Remove the lid for the last quarter of an hour of cooking to brown tl chicken. Serve hot. Eat with salads or cooked vegetables or pilaw.

An alternative method : Joint the chicken and wash, but leave the skin on. Place tl chicken pieces alongside each other. Add potatoes and onions as required (optiona Sprinkle with ginger, tumeric, salt and pepper, adding the cardimum pods and clove Pour on the oil or chicken fat but do not add any water. Cover, and cook for three quarte of an hour on the middle shelf of a preheated oven on 400° Reg. 6. Remove the lid ai continue cooking for another quarter of an hour or until the chicken browns.

Serve as above.

One of our cooks prepared hurikebab in the traditional way, without onions potatoes. When the chicken was cooked, two large onions would be sliced thickly rounds and glazed in the hurikebab oil or fat and heaped over the chicken with shredde capsicums and cucumber slices.

For a traditional chicken sandwich, shred the cold hurikebab chicken. Mix tl potatoes with Dhunia Chutney, see above, add the chicken and use as a filling.

Alternatively, substitute the Dhunia chutney with Kashmiri pickle and use as filling.

Beef or Lamb Hurikebab

Prepare *3 lbs of stewing beef or lamb* by cutting into mouth sized pieces and
imming the fat. Wash and leave to drain.

Heat *4 tablespoons of vegetable oil.* Add *1 dessertspoon of grated or
nely chopped fresh ginger, 2 cloves of grated garlic, 1 medium sized
aion finely chopped.* Fry until the mixture is golden brown and considerably
duced. Then add *1 teaspoon of turmeric powder, 1 stick of cinnamon, 3
oves and 3 cardimum pods.* Mix thoroughly. Add the meat to this mixture and seal
ver a hot flame. Reduce to medium heat and cook with the lid on for half an hour. By
is time the juices should have been absorbed into the meat . Add peeled potatoes and
nions as required and sprinkle with *1 teaspoon salt and pepper to taste.* Add tepid
ater to just cover the level of the meat and cook for half an hour uncovered on a very
w light, by which time the water should have absorbed. The meat should be moist and
ot too dry.

Serve hot with a cooked vegetable or bhaji.

Hurikebabed Shooftas

Prepare the shooftas as shown above but do not cook them. Instead, proceed in this
ay.

Heat *2 tablespoons of vegetable oil* until it just begins to smoke. Then add and stir
y *1 teaspoon of grated ginger, $\frac{1}{2}$ teaspoon of grated garlic, $\frac{1}{2}$ teaspoon turmeric
owder, 2 cloves, 2 cardimum pods, $\frac{1}{2}$ teaspoon cinnamon powder, $\frac{1}{2}$ teaspoon of
rated nutmeg* until the aroma rises.

Pour this into a wide bottomed saucepan and lower the prepared shooftas into it,
dding *6 or 8 small whole potatoes, 6 or 8 shallots or small onions left
hole, and 3 carrots* cut into wedges.

Cover and bake on gas mark 5 for an hour in a preheated oven. Remove the cover
r the last quarter of an hour.

Serve hot with relishes.

Incree

Since the Jews in Bombay and Cochin had facilities for the slaughter of lar[g]
animals they were able to make dishes which originated in Baghadad for which meat w[as]
essential. Dishes such as Incree were discontinued in Calcutta. Daisy Iny records a di[sh]
called Bamiah Hamudh from Baghdad which is very similar to what the Cochin Je[ws]
describe as Incree.

Saute *1 1b of onions finely sliced in 2 tablespoons of vegetable o[il]*.
Trim the fat from $2\frac{1}{2}$ *1bs of lamb* and cut into mouth sized pieces. Add this to the onio[ns]
and seal the meat over a high flame, ensuring the pieces are browned all over. Shred [a]
large red pepper and add this to the meat together with *2 tablespoons of chopped cele[ry]
leaves and 3 tablespoons of tomato puree.* Add *1 pint of hot water,* bring to the boil a[nd]
simmer.

When the meat is tender add *1 1b of lady's fingers* which have been topped a[nd]
tailed, slit down one side and checked for imperfections . Bring this to the boil and simm[er]
for 20 minutes or until the vegetable is cooked but firm.

Add the *juice of 2 lemons and sugar to taste.* Boil for another couple of minut[es]
and serve hot.

Incree may be eaten with pilaw or boiled rice.

A variation of Incree is to substitute fried aubergine for the lady's fingers, [in]
which case there is no need for further cooking once the vegetable is added. Simply cov[er]
the meat with the fried aubergine, add the lemon juice and sugar, bring to the boil and ser[ve]
straight away.

Ingree

This dish from Bombay was very popular and became a favourite for festivals and Friday nights. Chop and glaze *a small onion in 2 tablespoons of vegetable oil.* Add *1 lb of minced chicken, or beef, $\frac{1}{2}$ teaspoon of turmeric powder, 1 teaspoon of salt and pepper to taste.* Simmer in an uncovered saucepan for about half an hour or until the chicken has almost cooked through. The mince should be pressed down with a fork from time to time.

Set aside.

Coat the bottom of a wide saucepan with *vegetable oil. Slice potatoes* fairly thick and line the bottom of the saucepan. Pour the cooked mince over the potatoes and cover the mince with fairly thick slices of aubergine which have been salted for 20 minutes and drained. Cover the aubergine with *thick slices of tomatoes.* Slice a mixture of *green, yellow and red pepers* and sprinkle this over the tomatoes. Slice *a fresh lemon* and spread over the top.

Prepare a gravy by mixing $\frac{1}{2}$ *cup of vegetable oil with 4 tablespoons of vinegar, the juice of a lemon, 1 teaspoon of grated ginger and half a teaspoon of grated garlic. Add salt and pepper to taste.*

Pour the gravy over the layers of vegatables and minced chicken and bake in a moderately hot oven – gas mark 4 – middle shelf for an hour.

Garnish with *chopped coriander leaves* and serve hot.

This dish is also tasty when cold and therefore convenient for Saturday lunch.

Kababdus

Joint a *4 lb chicken,* wash and dry pieces and set aside.

Saute *3 large onions* which have been finely sliced in *6 tablespoons of vegetable oil.* When the onions are golden, add the chicken pieces and stir fry for five minutes on medium flame. Add $\frac{1}{2}$ *cup of cold water* and *either the juice of half a lemon, or preferably, a teaspoon of tamarind paste, 3 cloves, 3 cardimum pods, 1 teaspoon fresh ginger, crushed or grated, 1 teaspoon grated garlic, 1 teaspoon salt, $\frac{1}{2}$ teaspoon turmeric powder.* Stir over moderate heat until the water is reduced.

Cover and bake in preheated oven on gas mark 6, for an hour, or until the chicken is tender.

Serve hot with rice or pilaw.

Meat Keema

This was a popular dish in Bombay and was made with minced lamb, but minced beef or chicken would do just as well.

Fry *1 1b of minced meat in 3 tablespoons of vegetable oil* until it is cooked through Let it stand.

Chop fine *3 large onions* and add it to the mince together with *1 cup of shredded white cabbage, 1 cup of chopped carrots, 1 cup of chopped celery stalks and leaves 2 teaspoons grated ginger, $\frac{1}{2}$ teaspoon grated garlic, $\frac{1}{2}$ teaspoon turmeric powder, and a few green chillies (optional).* Mix thoroughly and cook, uncovered, in a preheated oven on gas mark 4 for 45 minutes.

Remove from the oven.

Garnish with chopped coriander leaves and serve hot with relishes.

Koofta Curry

Koofta is a small meat ball made from minced chicken, veal or beef. This is cooked a curry sauce and with local modifications is popular in Northern India.

To prepare the sauce : Grate *4 large onions* and brown in *8 tablespoons of vegetable l*. Add *1 cup of water* and bring to the boil. Simmer and add *3 tablespoons of garam asala* (this includes equal quantities of cumin powder, coriander powder, ground nnamon and chillie powder. If necessary the chillie may be omitted, in which case do it use prepared garam masala). Use *1 dessertspoon of tamarind paste or the juice of marind,* ie soak the seeds in boiling water for five minutes, stir and strain. Alternatively, se the *juice of 1 lemon.* Add *salt and pepper to taste.*

To prepare the koofta : Use *1 $\frac{1}{2}$ lbs of minced chicken, veal or beef* for four enerous portions. Mix with *2 medium sized onions* which have been sliced and browned, *small egg, 1 thick slice of white bread which has been trimmed,* soaked in water, and rumbled, or *2 tablespoons of breadcrubs or matzo-meal.* Add *$\frac{1}{2}$ teaspoon turmeric, tablespoons coriander powder, 1 tablespoon cumin powder. Salt and pepper to taste.* Iix thoroughly. Wet your hands and take a small portion, the size of a small egg, and ake into a ball. Drop into the hot sauce. Continue until the mixture has been completely sed in this way.

Simmer for half an hour or until the kooftas are cooked through.

A heavy, wide–bottomed saucepan is most satisfactory to prepare this dish to nsure all the kooftas are cooked in the sauce.

Serve hot, with rice or pilaw.

Traditionally, the koofta curry was served with a topping of fried potatoes which ad been finely sliced. This is an optional extra.

Some people prefer their curries lighter and less highly spiced, in which case the auce may be prepared by frying sliced rather than grated onions. When the onions are golden brown, set aside one tablespoon for the kooftas and add *$\frac{3}{4}$ pint of cold water.* ring it to the boil and simmer to reduce to half the bulk. Then add *1 tablespoon of oriander powder, a pinch of turmeric and chillie powder* (optional). Stir for a couple f minutes and add the meat or chicken balls. The kooftas may be made as shown above. ut the cumin powder may be left out and fewer onions added to the mixture.

Mango and Chicken Dopyasa

The mangoes used for this dish are the small green, sour, cooking or pickling varie(
imported from India and East Africa. The traditonal way of preparing chicken, mainly i
an onion sauce, has been elaborated with the use of the cooking mangoes which ar
indigenous to India rather than to the Middle East.

Clean and joint *a 5 lb roasting ckicken.* Remove the skin and set aside. Saute
large onions finely chopped in *4 tablespoons of vegetable or sunflower oil or 3 ozs (
chicken fat. Add 1 dessertspoon of grated ginger, $\frac{1}{2}$ dessertspoon of grated garli(
1 teaspoon turmeric powder, 1 teaspoon salt, pepper to taste, 3 cloves and 4 cardimu.
pods.* Stir and mix thoroughly with $\frac{1}{2}$ *cup water.* Add the chicken and stir well. Cove
bring to the boil and then simmer for about a quarter of an hour. Meanwhile, peel and c
in halves *2 lbs of green mangoes* (the soft seed at the centre should be discarded) an
2 large potatoes, peeled and cut in cubes. Add this and $\frac{1}{2}$ *pint of water* to the chicke
bring to the boil and cover.

Finish cooking in a preheated oven on gas mark 4, middle shelf for an hour. Ha
way through the cooking stir to ensure the ingredients are thorughly blended and the sau(
thickened with the potatoes. If necessary a little water may be added.

When the chicken is tender serve hot, on a bed of rice or pilaw.

Carrot Meetah

Peel and shred $2\frac{1}{2}$ *lbs of carrots* and fry in *4 tablespoons of vegetable oil* over a ow flame. When the carrots become reduced add *1 teaspoon of salt and $\frac{1}{2}$ teaspoon of urmeric.* Stir fry again for a few minutes. Set aside.

Saute *1 large onion* finely sliced. When the onions are glazed add a *4 lb jointed hicken, $\frac{1}{2}$ teaspoon turmeric, 3 cloves and 2 cardimum, and salt and pepper to taste, teaspoon of grated ginger and $\frac{1}{2}$ teaspoon of garlic.* Stir fry.

Add the carrots together with *half a pint of water,* bring to the boil and then simmer or half an hour until the chicken becomes somewhat tender. Meanwhile, prepare the oobas or kooftas.

Prepare koobas or kooftas by mincing the *breast of chicken—one half* should be ufficent– and adding *1 tablespoon chopped mint, a small chopped onion which should e sprinkled with salt* and left to stand for a quarter of an hour and then squeezed dry, nd *pepper to taste.* Wet your hands and make small balls from the mixture. For those who ant kooftas, drop these straight into the chicken and carrots. For koobas, the kooftas hould be encased with a shell made from a stiff dough made with *ground rice, a little easoning* and a spoonful of the koofta mixture, together with *just sufficient water to bind* t together.

Simmer for another half an hour by which time the chicken and koobas or kooftas hould be tender. If there is too much juice then this may be reduced over a high flame or a few minutes.

Add the *juice of 1 lemon, 2 teaspoons of sugar* and stir.

Serve with rice.

Some people prepare this meetah without the kooftas or koobas, in which case the :ooking may be completed in the oven without adding the half pint of water.

t is also possible to prepare this dish without the chicken, i.e. using the vegetables and :oobas or kooftas.

The range of meetahs are cooked somewhat differently in Bombay where they do 1ot use ginger and garlic but do use, instead, *2 sticks of cinnamon and a scrape of grated 1utmeg.* They also add *1 tablespoon of uncooked white rice* to the particular vegetable 1sed.

Lubia Meetah

Lubia or black-eyed bean is used traditionally but may be substituted by any oth
green bean. The taste will vary somewhat.

Saute *a large onion* finely sliced. When the onions are glazed add *2 lbs of bea*
which have been chopped, $\frac{1}{2}$ teaspoon of turmeric, 3 cloves, 2 cardimum, 1 teaspoo
grated garlic, 1 teaspoon of grated ginger. Stir fry for five minutes. Add the pieces o
$4\frac{1}{2}$ *lb jointed chicken with $\frac{1}{2}$ pint of water.* Stir and reduce over a high flame.

When the water has been absorbed add another $\frac{1}{2}$ pint of water and prepare th
koobas or kooftas.

Mince the *breast of half a chicken* and add *1 tablespoon of chopped fres*
mint leaves, a small chopped onion which should be sprinkled with sa
left to stand for a quarter of an hour and then squeezed dry, and *pepper to taste.*

Make small balls from the mixture with wet hands. For those who want koofta
drop them straight into the chicken and beans. For those who want koobas, the koofta
should be encased with a shell made from a stiff dough made with *ground rice, a litt*
seasoning and a spoonful of the koofta mixture with just enough water
bind it together.

Simmer for another half an hour by which time the chicken and koobas or kooft
should be tender. If there is too much juice this can be reduced over a high flame for a fe
minutes.

Serve with rice.

Other chopped vegetables may be used instead of beans, such as pumpkin, f
example. Meetah may be prepared with vegetables and koobas or kooftas only; or wi
vegetables and chicken pieces only. In our family it was usual to include vegetables wi
both the jointed chicken and koobas.

Morwarchi

This is the Malayalam name for a chillie-hot chicken dish and comes from the community in Cochin.

Use *2 tablespoons of vegetable oil or chicken fat* to fry together *1 large chopped onion, 1 tablespoon chillie powder, $\frac{1}{2}$ tablespoon coriander powder, $\frac{1}{2}$ teaspoon turmeric powder, 4 fresh green chillies, salt and pepper to taste.* When the aroma rises, add *4 chopped tomatoes* and mix well with the above ingredients. Stir and continue frying until the tomatoes have cooked.

Add the pieces of a *4 lb roasting chicken* and mix thoroughly with the above ingredients. Add *1 cup of cold water,* bring this to the boil and reduce the liquid, stirring from time to time. Cover the saucepan and place on the middle shelf of a preheated oven on gas mark 6 for an hour or until the chicken is quite tender.

Dissolve *1 tablespoon of sugar in 3 tablespoons of vinegar* (wine vinegar will be more smooth) and adjust the sweet-sour quantities to taste. Pour this over the cooked chicken, mix thoroughly, and serve hot.

Morwarchi may be eaten with rice, pilaw or potatoes.

This dish is intended to be very hot so there would be little point in recommending the reduction or deletion of chillies.

Pacha

Pacha is stuffed stomach of lamb and was not part of the cuisine in Calcutta because lambs were seldom available there. However, I can remember people who were born and spent their early years in Baghdad who recalled this dish with longing. The community in Bombay were able to indulge their liking for pacha. Stomach of lamb is not available in this country but an alternative is stuffed breast of lamb. The stuffing of the original pacha was spiced rice and chopped meat. If breast of lamb is used then the addition of chopped meat may be unnecessary or could be reduced substantially.

Clean and trim the *breast of lamb (one large or two small ones)*. Season by rubbing in $\frac{1}{2}$ *teaspoon of turmeric and pepper to taste*. Salt is probably unnecessary for meat which has been bought from a kosher butcher or which has rested for an hour in salt at home.

Stuff the lamb with about $\frac{1}{2}$ *lb of finely chopped meat, 1 chopped tomato, 1 cup of washed and uncooked rice* flavoured with $\frac{1}{2}$ *teaspoon of turmeric, 3 pods of cardimum, 3 cloves, 1 stick of cinnamon, $\frac{1}{2}$ teaspoon of grated nutmeg, pepper and salt to taste*. Half a teaspoon of salt should be sufficient.

Ask the butcher to prepare the lamb for stuffing and rolling. When the pacha has been stuffed it should be tied to retain the stuffing.

Slice *3 large onions in rings* and place in a wide bottomed saucepan which has been very lightly greased. Cover the onions with fairly thick slices of tomatoes. Place the stuffed breast of lamb over the tomatoes and pierce the meat in a few places. Cover the lamb with water, bring to the boil and place in a preheated oven on gas mark 4 for $1\frac{1}{2}$ hours and then reduce the heat to gas mark 3 for another two hours or until the meat is tender. The meat should be oven cooked uncovered.

Serve hot. Cut in slices and cover with gravy and the onions and tomatoes.

Traditionally pacha was eaten with halba.

Spinach & Chicken Mahmoosa

Chop and glaze *a small onion,* in *2 tablespoons of vegetable oil.* Add *1 lb of inced chicken, $\frac{1}{2}$ teaspoon of turmeric powder and 1 teaspoon of salt and pepper to ste.* Simmer in an uncovered saucepan until the chicken is cooked through. This should ke about half an hour. To ensure that the mince does not stick together press it down with fork in the early stages of cooking.

Wash, dry and chop *1 lb of spinach leaves* and mix with the mince chicken. Add *eggs* and scramble with the spinach and mince.

Slice *3 aubergines* fairly thick, salt and leave to stand for 20 minutes. Drain, pat dry id fry in *3 tablespoons of vegetable oil.*

Arrange the spinach and chicken mince on a dish and surround it with the fried bergine.

This dish was popular in many homes for the Friday night meal in Bombay.

Stuffed Pigeon or Poulet

Clean and wash *a drawn pigeon or poulet,* sprinkle with *salt, pepper and a pinch f turmeric powder.* Allow a whole pigeon or half a poulet per person.

To stuff a single pigeon or poulet use *$\frac{1}{4}$ lb minced chicken, veal or lamb, 1 small nion chopped fine, 1 oz cooked white rice, 1 teaspoon cumin powder, 2 teaspoons oriander powder, 2 grated cloves of garlic, $\frac{1}{2}$ teaspoon grated fresh ginger (or ginger owder), 2 cloves, 1 cardimum, 1 dessertspoon of vegetable oil.* Mix thoroughly.

Stuff the pigeon or poulet, place in a greased baking dish and bake on gas mark 6, iiddle shelf for half an hour or until the poultry is cooked and the skin browned.

Serve with a relish and vegetables.

Chicken Sumak

Slice **2 breasts of a 5 lb roasting chicken,** score and rub with **salt, pepper** a $\frac{1}{2}$ **teaspoon of turmeric powder.** Fry in **4 tablespoons of vegetable oil.** Set aside.

In the same oil fry **2 large onions** cut in rings till golden. Set aside. In the same glaze **2 chopped celery stalks with the leaves.**

Arrange pieces of **pitta bread** as a substitute for sayeed bread on a large baking tr and spread the onions and celery over them evenly. Place the fried chicken slices over the and sprinkle with **2 teaspoons of sumak powder.** Sumak should be available in all Midd Eastern grocery stores. Alternatively, lemboo basra may be used.

Place this in the oven on gas mark 3 middle shelf for 20 minutes, and serve ho This delicious dish comes from Bombay.

Tass Kebab

The ingredients for this dish are built up in layers and since each layer has to be prepared separately it is time consuming, but delicious. Those who are familiar with Middle Eastern cooking will know that this method of preparation is indigenous to that part of the world.

The layers are made up of onions, tomatoes, potatoes and slices of breast of chicken or minced chicken or meat. However, considerable flexibility can be used and here are some suggestions: Onions, chicken slices, potatoes, almonds and raisins, or onions, tomatoes, aubergine slices and chicken slices.

Prepare the *onions* by cutting them in round slices (not too thin), saute and set aside. In the same *oil, enough to cover the bottom of a frying pan,* saute the *potatoes,* also cut in round slices (and again not too thin) until cooked but not at all crisp. Drain and set aside. Cut *fresh tomatoes* into rounds and set aside. *Thin slices of breast of chicken* should be cored and sprinkled with *salt, pepper, a generous pinch of turmeric, and a light coating of ginger powder.* Fry until sealed on both sides, but not browned. Chicken slices may be substituted by minced chicken or minced veal, but prepared in the same way as the chicken slices.

If raisins are used they should be fried in a litle oil until they plump up. Almonds should be blanched, cut in slivers, and gently fried but drained before they turn golden.

Take a heavy saucepan and grease the bottom generously with vegetable oil. This for the final preparation and here too there are alternatives. Either prepare the layers in portions or separate little rounds, which makes the dish easy to serve, or spread each layer to cover the saucepan completely all round.

First the onions go in then the potatoes, tomatoes, chicken and again potatoes and onions, ending with the tomatoes. Alternatively, onions, chicken, potatoes, almonds and raisins.

Finally, squeeze the *juice of a lemon,* mix with *a teaspoon of sugar* until the sugar is dissolved and sprinkle all over.

Bake on gas mark 6, middle shelf or in a moderately hot oven until the ingredients are cooked through. This should take approximately three quarters of an hour. Serve hot with a green salad.

The quantities used will depend on the portions to be served. For each portion, calculate on one small onion, one medium - sized potato, one large tomato and a generous slice of chicken. If almonds and raisins are to be used, and this is a traditional festive touch, one dessertspoon of almonds and one dessertspoon of raisins should be sufficient.

Vegetable Curry

Grate *2 large onions* and fry in *4 tablespoons of vegetable oil* until golden brow
This onion sauce should then be spiced with *2 teaspoons of coriander powder, 1 teaspoo*
of cumin powder, 2 cloves, 2 cardimum pods, half a teaspoon of turmeric powder, a
salt and pepper to taste.

Any vegetable or combination of vegetables, similar to those suggested for bhaj
can be added to the sauce, mixed thoroughly and stir fried for two minutes.

Cover the saucepan and bake in a preheated oven on gas mark 5, middle shelf f
about three quarters of an hour, or until the vegetables are cooked through. The preci
timing will vary with the vegetables selected.

For variation, add *fresh or canned tomatoes* to the onion sauce. *4 ozs* would
sufficient for the 2 large onions.

A sweet - sour curry can be made by adding *1 teaspoon of sugar to the juice of h*
a lemon, or a little tamarind water.

Fish Arook

Unlike murug arook, fish arook is a dry dish, either boiled or fried. Essentially t
same as murug arook, in that it consists of a filling, encased in a coat, fish is substitut
by chicken but the other ingredients are unchanged.

The method of cooking is also the same except that instead of boiling the arook
stock, it is boiled in water and either served straight out of the pan or boiled, cooled, a
subsequently fried in deep oil for a few minutes until the arook becomes a golden brov
colour. It should then be drained and eaten hot.

Arook forms a complete and delicious meal in its own right and is not traditiona
eaten with any other foods.

Fish Curry

Allow $\frac{1}{2}$ *lb of fish per person.* Cut the fish in portions, wash, dry and *sprinkle with* *lt and a pinch of turmeric.* Set the fish aside.

Slice *1 large Spanish onion.* Saute in *2 tablespoons of vegetable oil.* Add *3 large* *oves of crushed garlic* and *1 teaspoon of grated ginger.* Season with *1 teaspoon of salt,* *teaspoon of turmeric, and pepper to taste.* Mix thoroughly. On a low light add *14 ozs* *f fresh or tinned tomatoes.* Simmer until the tomatoes are reduced to a fairly thick sauce. dd *3 teaspoons of cumin powder, 5 teaspoons of coriander powder, 2 teaspoons* *f crushed mustards seeds, 2 cloves, 3 cardimum pods, chillie powder to taste* and *tablespoons of malt vinegar.* Mix thoroughly and simmer for five minutes. When the uce is prepared add the portions of fish.

Cover and simmer until the fish is cooked through and tender. Care should be taken ot to overcook so that the flesh does not break up.

Serve hot on a bed of rice or pilaw.

Black Seed Fish Curry

The 'black seed' referred to here is called 'koolonji' by its Indian name, and lthough onion seed is a misnomer, it is nevertheless commonly used. This particular urry was developed by one of our cooks and shows how instrumental they were in xpanding our Baghdadi repertoire.

Grate *2 large onions* and fry this in *4 dessertspoons of vegetable oil.* When glazed, dd $\frac{1}{2}$ *teaspoon of turmeric powder, salt and pepper to taste and 1 chopped green chillie* optional). Add $\frac{1}{2}$ *pint of cold water* and bring this to the boil. Then place *4 fillets* *f white fish* into the sauce and sprinkle *2 dessertspoons of coriander powder,* *dessertspoon of cumin powder and 1 tablespoon of 'black seeds'* preferably ground. 'over and simmer until the fish is cooked through. Adjust the seasoning and serve hot vith rice or pilaw.

Fish and Coconut Curry

This dish comes from Cochin where fresh fish and coconuts are both in plentiful supply.

Use *2 tablespoons of vegetable oil* to fry together *1 large chopped onion, 3 cloves of garlic* chopped fine or grated, *1 teaspoon of root ginger* also chopped fine or grated, $\frac{1}{2}$ *teaspoon turmeric powder, 1 teaspoon coriander powder*. Stir until the aroma rises. Then add *1 oz of fresh or dried curry leaves , 1 cup of cold water,* and *1 grated coconut.* Fresh coconuts are not difficult to find and these can be grated easily in a food processor. Alternatively use 8 ozs of fine dessicated coconut and mix this with just enough water to dampen the coconut. Bring this to the boil.

In the meantime wash and pat dry *2 lbs of white fish.* Sprinkle with $\frac{1}{2}$ *teaspoon of salt,* $\frac{1}{2}$ *teaspoon of turmeric powder, pepper* and allow this to stand for 20 to 30 minutes. Wipe dry again, coat lightly with *plain flour* and deep fry in hot *vegetable oil.*

Place the fried fish in the coconut sauce and bring to the boil. Adjust the seasoning. Serve hot with boiled rice and fried aubergine.

If preferred, the fried aubergine may be added to the coconut sauce with the fried fish.

Fish and Peas Meetah

Saute *1 medium sized onion* in *3 tablespoons of vegetable oil.* When the onions are glazed add $\frac{1}{2}$ *teaspoon of turmeric,* $2\frac{1}{2}$ *lbs of peas, salt and pepper to taste.* Stir fry for two or three minutes. Add *1 pint of cold water,* bring it to the boil and simmer.

In the meantime prepare fish koobas or kooftas by mixing *2 lbs of minced white fish, 1 teaspoon of freshly grated ginger, 4 cloves of garlic and 1 chopped onion.* It preferable to chop the onion, sprinkle it with salt and let it stand for at least 20 minutes before squeeze drying and adding it to the koofta mixture. For the kooba casing mix $\frac{1}{2}$ lb *of ground rice,* $\frac{1}{2}$ *teaspoon of salt and enough cold water to make a stiff dough.*

Lower the koobas gently into the simmering liquid, cover and continue to boil for ten minutes until the kooba casing begins to harden. Add *2 tablespoons of chopped coriander leaves* and continue to simmer for another 10 minutes, or until the liquid is reduced. Serve hot with rice or pilaw.

Fish Saloon

Any white fish is suitable for this dish which is cooked in an onion and tomato uce. Allow half a pound of fish per person.

Wash and cut into portions, *3 lbs of fish* filleted but with the skin left on. Chop very ie, or liquidise *2 large onions* and saute over low heat for 15 or 20 minutes until golden. :ld $\frac{1}{2}$ *teaspoon crushed garlic*, $\frac{1}{2}$ *teaspoon turmeric, 1 teaspoon salt and pepper to ste.* Mix thoroughly and add *1 lb chopped tomatoes - fresh or canned.* Crush the matoes into the onion mixture and simmer until the tomatoes are cooked through. Add *tablespoons of tomato paste dissolved in half a cup of warm water together* 'th $\frac{1}{2}$ *teaspoon of sugar. Blend thoroughly, add the fish, together with 5 or 6 curry* aves *and cover.* Curry leaves can be bought fresh, then dried for a few days in an airing pboard and stored almost indefinitely in a sterilised jar. The curry leaves are not sential but add a distinctive flavour and is the traditional way of preparation.

When the fish has cooked through, 30 minutes slow cooking should be sufficient, rve hot on a bed of rice or pilaw. Baked potatoes may be used instead of rice if this is eferred.

Polychul

This fish dish was traditionally made with mackerel in Cochin but any white fis may be substituted.

Wash *four portions of mackerel,* pat dry and score the fish diagonally several tim on both sides. The flesh should be scored right down to the bone. Sprinkle with $\frac{1}{2}$ *teaspo of salt, $\frac{1}{2}$ teaspoon of turmeric powder and pepper to taste.* Let the fish stand for 20 30 minutes. Pat dry again, dust on both sides with *plain flour* and deep fry in hot *vegetab oil.* Coconut oil was used traditionally in Cochin but other vegetable or seed oils are mo delicately flavoured. Set aside. If this is to be served hot, cover and keep warm.

In the same oil used to fry the fish add *1 large grated onion, 3 grated cloves garlic, $\frac{1}{2}$ teaspoon of grated root ginger, fresh green chillies chopped fine - to taste.* F over a high flame until the aroma rises, cool and add *1 oz fresh or dried curry leav and $\frac{1}{2}$ pint of tamarind water.*

The pulp and tamarind seeds are soaked in boiling water and strained through sieve when it has cooled. Alternatively, buy tamarind paste and dissolve 2 teaspoons boiling water. Lemon juice may be used as a substitute for tamarind water, although t consistency and colour will be different from the authentic dish. Bring this to the boil a simmer for five minutes. Season with *salt and pepper* to taste.

Pour the sauce over the fish and serve hot or cold.

In Cochin this dish was served cold over a bed of hot kitchree.

Stuffed fish or Fish Furruce

Clean and gut a *fish weighing 3 lbs.*

For the stuffing : Chop fine *a large onion.* Add *2 cloves of grate garlic, $\frac{1}{2}$ teaspoon of turmeric, 1 tablespoon of chopped coriander leaves* (or parsley salt and pepper to taste, and the juice of $\frac{1}{2}$ lemon.* Mix thoroughly with *2 tablespoo of vegetable oil a*nd stuff the fish.

Grease the bottom of a baking dish, place the fish on it and pour a trickle of oil ov the surface of the fish.

Bake in a moderately hot oven, gas mark 4, middle shelf, for 40 minutes or until t fish has a golden-brown tinge.

Skin the fish, place on a warm plate, pour over the juice of $\frac{1}{2}$ *lemon,* garnish wi *coriander leaves* and serve with any one of a range of bhartas and relishes.

Baked Goodies

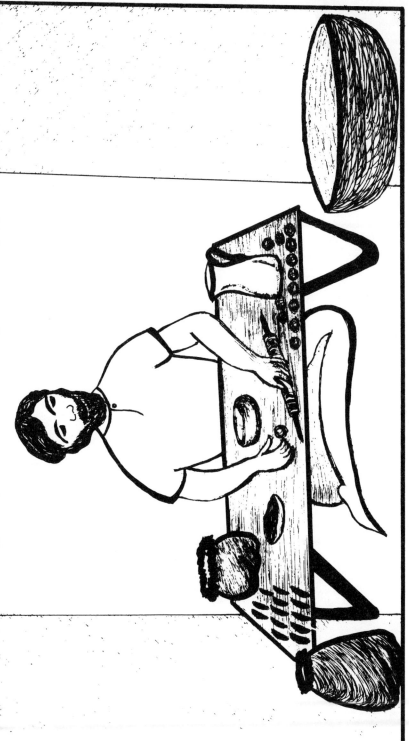

The itinerant baker

Baked Goodies

Baked goodies were not generally made at home in Calcutta, partly because oven ooking was not easily accessible and partly because there were excellent confectioners the community. In addition there were bakers who would come to the home and spend ours preparing a range of goodies. As a child I remember being wrapt in fascination as e baker would prepare batch after batch of cacas, babas and sumoosucks. My admiration as sometimes rewarded with minature versions of his goodies. He then carried verything off in an enormous basket balanced finely on his head, to his bakery. He would turn the same evening with freshly baked goodies, to a warm welcome from the family.

Almond Macaroons

Mix *1 lb of finely ground sweet almonds* with *8 ozs of caster sugar and 4 ozs of icing sugar. 1 teaspoonful of ground cinnamon* is optional. Add *1 teaspoon of essence of vanilla and a few drops of essence of almond.* Beat *an egg* lightly, the yolk and the white together, and add this gradually to the other ingredients. The almonds should have a doughlike consistency and not be tacky. Use as much egg as is necessary to get the consistency right.

Wet your hands and make a ball out of one heaped teaspoon of the mixture. Decorate the top with a split almond. Continue in this way, placing the macaroons on tray lined with baking paper.

Bake in a preheated oven on gas mark 4, for 20 to 30 minutes. The macaroon should be a pale golden colour and the underneath should just turn golden to ensure the are cooked through.

Almond Marzipan

The almond 'dough' is made in exactly the same way as the macaroons above except that only icing sugar should be used to make up the entire quantity of 12 ozs. The consistency should be dry but malleable. Divide the mixture into batches and add a few drops of food colour into each batch - varying the colours. Shape into fruit, multi-coloured balls, or as your imagination takes you and decorate with a mixture of split blanched almonds, walnuts, cherries, dates or chocolate buttons.

Almond Rings

Mix *8 ozs ground almonds* with *6 ozs of caster sugar*. Whip the *whites of 2 eggs* and mix with the almonds and sugar. Add *½ teaspoon essence of almond and ½ teaspoon essence of vanilla* together with *1 tablespoon of fresh lemon juice*. The mixture should have a tacky consistency.

Dampen an icing bag and fix with a large rosette head. Put the mixture into the bag and pipe into concentric circles. Two or three circles is sufficient, depending on the size desired.

Bake in a preheated oven on the middle shelf on gas mark 4 for 30 minutes. Watch the baking carefully after the first 20 minutes. The outside of the almond rings should be golden brown.

Almond rings have a crunchy exterior and are soft at the centre.

Almond Sumoosucks

Make the pastry by mixing *12 ozs self-raising flour, 1 teaspoon sugar dissolved ¾ cup of tepid water, 4 ozs margarine, a pinch of salt*. Mix by hand as it is quick and easy. The dough should stand at room temperature for at least 1 hour.

For the filling : Grind *½ lb of blanched almonds to a crumbly rather than powdered consistency*. Add *6oz caster sugar* and bind with a *little egg* lightly beaten. Flavour with *tablespoons of rose water, or crushed seeds from 6 cardimum pods,* or both, depending on personal preference. If the mixture is moist dust with a little flour.

To assemble : Divide the pastry into equal portions, depending on the preferred size. Make into balls and roll out into circles. For a 4" long sumoosuck take a tablespoon of filling and place it on one side of the circle. Fold the other side over. Press the edges together and seal with a pastry wheel about a quarter of an inch away from the filling.

Bake on greaseproof paper in a preheated oven on the middle shelf gas mark 4 for 5 minutes. Cool.

Store in an air-tight container when cold.

Apam

This is a coconut flavoured cake. Dissolve a *7 oz cake of coconut cream* in *1 pint of water, or use a tin of coconut milk.* Bring to the boil and allow to simmer until the cake is completely dissolved. Add *2 cups of bread crumbs,* which is the traditional mix or substitute with mazo meal. Beat in *3 eggs* and add *1 cap of essence of vanilla.* Stir in $\frac{1}{2}$ *cup of jagury* called "gur" in Hindi, which is the traditional ingredient, or substitute with either golden syrup or halek (see below) which is delicious and which complements the coconut flavour admirably. Alternatively, use brown sugar.

Oil a pie dish and bake on gas mark 4 for 45 minutes on the middle shelf of preheated oven. Carry out a skewer test to ensure the apam has cooked through.

The top of the apam may be sprinkled with *slivers of almonds.*

Savoury Biscuit

This biscuit is probably an adapted form of Caca, using "koolonji", sometimes called onion seeds, to flavour short pastry.

Make a dough with *8 ozs of self-raising flour, 2 ozs margarine, 2 tablespoons vegetable oil, 1 teaspoon "koolonji", $\frac{1}{2}$ teaspoon sugar, $\frac{1}{2}$ teaspoon salt* with enough *lukewarm water* to bind the dough. Cover, and allow to stand for about an hour at least.

Roll out the pastry and stamp out circles roughly 3" in diameter. Roll each circle again in one direction to get the shape of an elongated circle. The pastry should not be rolled out too thin.

Place on a baking sheet in a preheated oven on gas mark 4, middle shelf and bake for 20 - 30 minutes or until the biscuits are golden brown.

Cool and store in an airtight container.

This savoury biscuit was usually served with a cup of tea but it will go equally well with cheese and wine.

Cacas

This is a very popular savoury biscuit, usually served with a cup of tea. Flavoured ith carraway or fennel seeds it could be served with drinks.

Each family probably has its own favourite dough recipe; I am including two here, 1e for a crumbly and one for a firmer consistency.

For a crumbly consistency: Make a dough with *12 ozs self raising white flour, teaspoon sugar dissolved in $\frac{3}{4}$ cup of tepid water, a pinch of salt, 2 ozs margarine, tablespoons vegetable or sunflower oil.* Add *1 teaspoon carraway or fennel seeds* ptional). The dough should be soft but firm.

For a firm consistency : *12 ozs self raising white flour, 1 teaspoon salt, 1 teaspoon ıgar dissolved in $\frac{3}{4}$ cup tepid water, 4 ozs margarine.* Make a dough which should be ıft but quite firm.

The dough is very quick and easy to make by hand using either recipe. Cover and low to stand at room temperature for 1 hour.

Divide the dough into small balls, about the size of a walnut. Roll each ball between 1e palms of your hands so that the dough tapers into a plain candle shape about 1 cm. in ameter and 5 - 6 cms long. Join the two ends to form a circle by overlapping and pinching gether the first and last cm.

Bake in a preheated oven on the middle shelf, gas mark 5 for 20 minutes or until 1e cacas just turn a pale gold colour. Cacas need to be watched towards the end of the aking as they may need to be repositioned if the temperature in the oven is not even.

Store in an air-tight container when cold.

Many books on Middle Eastern cooking suggest that "cacas" in one form or another widely made in those regions. The names vary from place to place, as do the ingredients, ut basically there is a similarity in this savoury biscuit which is sometimes flavoured ith dried herb seeds.

Cheese Cakes

Cheese cakes are made in individual moulds, either using a conventional small jar tart pan or the larger moulds in Yorkshire Pudding pans, which is the size in which the were traditionally made.

Like cheese cakes in the West, these cakes are also comprised of a base or cup, th cheese filling itself, and the topping.

For the base : Mix together *6 oz self raising flour, 2 ozs margarine, ½ teaspoo sugar, a small pinch of salt and ¼ cup of lukewarm water* (or sufficient to hold the doug together). The pastry should be covered and allowed to rest for about half an hour.

The cheese filling : This is an essentially sweet cake and the savoury traces of th cheese are consequently disguised. Mix together, *8 oz of cooking or curd cheese, 2 eg yolks, 1 egg white stiffly beaten, ¾ cup caster sugar, 1 ½ caps essence of vanilla.*

To assemble the cake : Roll out the pastry until it is fine and cut out circles to fit th bottom of the tart pan. This is the pastry case. Fill the pastry case with the cheese fillin almost to the top.

The topping : The remaining *egg white* should then be very lighly beaten; as th froth forms it should be lifted on to each cake, covering it to the very edges. Continue t beat the egg white lighly, transferring the froth to each cake as it forms. When each cak is covered with the lighly beaten egg white, *sprinkle generously with granulated suga* The sugar should not be blended with the egg white.

Bake in a moderate pre-heated oven, gas mark 5, top shelf, for 20 - 30 minutes, c until the top is a pale brown colour.

This mixture should produce 10 large cheese cakes. The cakes should keep well fo at least a week if stored in an air tight container in a cool place.

Cheese Sticks

Cheese sticks are very quick and easy to prepare and make an excellent snack with inks.

Sift *6 ozs self raising flour* and add $\frac{1}{2}$ *teaspoon salt*, $\frac{1}{2}$ *teaspoon mustard powder, teaspoon paprika.* Rub in *3 ozs butter and 4 ozs finely grated cheese* (a hard white riety is best). Add *2 egg yolks and 1 tablespoon of cold water* to firm up the dough. ix thoroughly, knead gently on a floured board and allow to stand for an hour in the idge.

Roll out the dough fairly thick. Cut in strips about 4" long x $\frac{3}{4}$" wide (or as preferred) id bake in a preheated oven, middle shelf, in a greased baking tin on gas mark 6 for 10 inutes or until golden brown.

Store in an air-tight container when cold.

Cheese Sumoosucks

This is a cheese pastie. To prepare the cheese filling. Grate *1 lb of a hard whit* *cheese* (such as Cheddar or Gouda). *Sprinkle lightly with salt and add 2 sma* *lightly beaten eggs. Sprinkle with self raising flour.* Just enough to help th filling rise in baking and to ensure that the cheese and egg mixture is reasonably firm. S aside.

For the pastry, make a dough with *12 ozs of self raising flour, 1 teaspoo* *of salt, 1 teaspoon of sugar dissolved in $\frac{3}{4}$ cup of tepid water, 2 ozs of margarine an* *4 tablespoons of vegetable oil.* Cover and allow to stand at room temperature for 1 hou

Divide the dough into small balls - about the size of a walnut.

Roll out each ball into a circle, place two teaspoons of the filling on one side of th circle and fold the other side over. Make sure the filling is about a quarter of an inch awa from the edges. Crimp and seal. Bake in a preheated oven, middle shelf on gas ma 4, for half an hour. Watch the baking after 20 minutes. The sumoosucks should be a lig golden colour and not brown.

It is clear from Daisy Iny's book that cheese sumoosucks were popular in Baghda and Claudia Roden's work suggests that it is known widely in Middle Eastern countrie

A variation on cheese sumoosucks, suggested by a friend, is to use the filling an add just enough self raising flour to it to make a stiff dough. Divide the cheese dough int balls the size of a walnut, place on a baking tray and bake as directed for sumoosucks. Th method cuts down on the flour used and is considerably labour-saving.

For another variation, not so labour-saving, make cheese puffs using the fillin suggested above with the casing made out of puff pastry, and place in a tart tray. Cov each one with a pastry lid and top with two strips of pastry, as in hot cross buns. Brus the lids with egg yolk and bake in a preheated oven, middle shelf on gas mark 6 for ha an hour or until the cheese puffs are golden brown. It is worth the effort and makes delicious party food.

Date Babas

This is a sweet-savoury biscuit with date filling.

For the pastry, mix *12ozs self raising white flour, a pinch of salt, 2 ozs margarine, 4 tablespoons vegetable or sunflower oil, 1 teaspoon sugar dissolved in $\frac{3}{4}$ cup of tepid water.* The dough should be soft but firm.

For the filling : chop *8 ozs stoned dates* and place in a frying pan with *a tablespoon of water* and *a tablespoon of vegetable oil.* Cook the dates until they are of a smooth consistency by pressing down with a fork over a low flame.

Be sure to cool the dates completely before filling the pastry otherwise the pastry will be soft rather than crisp.

Cut out 4" squares. Place a thin layer of dates over one square up to a quarter of an inch away from the edge. Cover with another 4" square of pastry, crimp and seal the edges. Pierce the top layer of pastry with a fork in two or three places, to allow the steam to escape while baking, and bake on greaseproof paper on the middle shelf on gas mark 5 in a preheated oven for 20 minutes.

The above quantity should produce 20 date babas.

Although it is not the traditional way, a few crushed walnuts may be added to the dates.

Kelicha

Kelicha is a savoury shortbread, which families who have suffered a bereavement in the previous year distribute to their relatives and friends just before the Fast of Tisha B'Av. The reason is that a blessing may be made in memory of the departed.

Knead *6 oz of self raising flour* with *4 ozs of margarine.* Add *1 teaspoon of salt* (or to taste). Some people add an egg to enrich the mixture but this is optional.

Allow the dough to stand for an hour. Then roll out onto a flat surface, about $\frac{1}{4}$" thick and cut out circles 4" in diameter.

Transfer the Kelicha on a greased baking tray and bake in a preheated oven on gas mark 6, until golden. This should take 20-30 minutes.

When cold, store in an air tight container.

Kooleecha

Kooleecha is a coconut based cookie. If it is to be mixed by hand, cream *4 ozs caster sugar and 2 ozs of unsalted butter.* When white, smooth and fluffy ad *4 ozs semolina (fine)* and blend with the butter and sugar. Moisten *6 oz dessicate coconut in one-third of a pint of milk.* Add this to the mixture together wi *1 capful of essence of vanilla.* Blend thoroughly.

If a food processor is used, all the above ingredients may be mixed at one time

Divide the mixture into 12 equal parts, roll each part into a ball, flatten and pla on a baking tray. Brush the top with a little vegetable oil.

The top of each kooleecha should be *lightly sprinkled with Koolonji or oni seeds.* This gives it its distinctive traditional flavour but poppy seeds may be used preferred.

Bake in a preheated oven on the top shelf at gas mark 7, for 20 minutes. T kooleechas should be golden brown.

Mulfoof

Mulfoof is a nut-filled pastry. The nearest I have seen to the pastry required is 'filo', ailable in Greek grocery shops. I use the thickness of three leaves at a time but for those ho are willing to make an acceptable pastry at home mix *12 ozs of self-raising hite flour, 1 teaspoon sugar* dissolved in $\frac{3}{4}$ *cup tepid water, a pinch of salt and 2 ozs argarine.* Let the dough stand at room temperature for an hour.

I know of three separate fillings for mulfoof -

Pistachio nut filling : Grind $\frac{1}{2}$ *pound of shelled pistachio nuts* to a crunchy nsistency and mix with *4 ozs caster sugar.* Flavour with *2 tablespoons of rose water.*

Almond filling : Substitute almonds for pistachio nuts.

Mixed nuts filling : Combine any nuts to taste, eg brazil nuts, walnuts, pecan nuts, c.

Mulfoof may be described as a crisp, dry strudle about 6" long and 1" in diameter. he pastry should be rolled out on a floured board and cut into strips 8" x 4". Line up the ling about half an inch from one edge. Turn the top and bottom ends in, to cover the ling at the ends, then roll the pastry over from one side to the other to form a casing.

Bake in a preheated oven, middle shelf, gas mark 4 for 10 minutes. The pastry ould just cook through and remain crisp.

Dust liberally with icing sugar when cool.

Store in an air tight container when cold.

Reference to Daisy Iny shows that Mulfoof, known by exactly the same name, and epared in very much the same way, has been retained in India for 200 years by the wish community. Much credit for this must go to the excellent confectioners who were le to make it available.

Nariel Ka Singara

This Cochini delicacy is very much an adaptation of Indian ingredients to an Ira
style of cooking. Singaras are three-cornered pasties usually filled with spiced vegetabl
or with meat, and fried. These coconut-filled pasties are baked.

For the pastry : Mix *12 ozs of self-raising white flour, 1 teaspoon sug
dissolved in $\frac{3}{4}$ cup of tepid water, 4 ozs margarine, and a pinch of salt.* Leave the dou
to stand at room temperature for at least an hour.

For the filling : Traditionally freshly grated coconut was used in this recipe, but fi
dessicated coconut will provide an acceptable substitute. *Mix 4 ozs of dessicat
coconut with 3 ozs of white sugar.* Add *2 tablespoons of rose water* to flavour a
moisten the mixture. The filling should be of a crumbly consistency. If necessary, a
a little cold water.

To assemble : Divide the pastry into equal portions. Roll each portion into a b
and then flatten and roll out into a circle about 4" - 5" in diameter. Shape into a cone. F
lightly with the coconut mixture and seal the cone by using the top of the pastry to ma
a lid.

Place the singaras on a baking tray in a preheated oven on the middle shelf on g
mark 4 for 25 minutes or until the singaras are golden. Cool and store in an air-tig
container.

Nulchatai

This cookie has a crunchy consistency and should look a little like rock cakes, but
e not quite so highly baked. Nulchatai should have a pale gold appearance and therefore
: removed from the oven as soon as the edges begin to darken.

Melt *4 ozs of margarine or unsalted butter* over a low flame. Add *1 cup
f sugar* and stir till the sugar is dissolved. Add *1 cup of self raising flour* and
hile still on a low heat stir until the mixture is quite smooth. Add *1 $\frac{3}{4}$ cup of semolina.*
ix thoroughly and add $\frac{1}{2}$ *cup of rose water.* Remove from the heat and work the
se water into the mixture. Line a baking tray with non-stick paper. Drop one tablespoon
f the mixture at wide intervals as it will spread while baking.

Smooth the top of the mixture with the back of a metal spoon or a palette knife. A
nall diamond pattern, repeated two or three times may be incised on the surface if you
ish to keep up a traditional detail. Brush the surface with oil.

Bake on gas mark 4 in a preheated oven, on the middle shelf for 30 minutes, but
atch it a little earlier.

When cool, turn out on a dish and serve. Nulchatai should keep well for several
ays in an air-tight container.

It is difficult to know the origins of nulchatai since there are many recipes for
milar cookies in Western cook books. The main difference between them is the variation
the balance of flour and semolina, or the use of flour exclusively in favour of semolina.
here is consequently a difference in consistency and the dough sometimes used for a
ariation on nulchatai is stiff and instead of being spooned on to a baking tray as suggested
ere, is made into balls which are then shaped in various ways and brushed over with oil
assist the browning process.

Pistachio Gateaux

This is a speciality of Nahoum & Sons, although the recipe here does not com
from the firm. I haven't seen it sold anywhere else in my travels and it would seem to l
an adaptation of Western style confectionery to the ingredients available and enjoyed b
people of the Middle East and India.

To make the sponge mixture in a food processor use *6 ozs self raising flou
5 ozs caster sugar, 3 ozs butter, 6 eggs and 3 or 4 drops of pistachio essenc*
Pistachio essence is not easily available in this country even in the most prestigiou
grocery shops. It is prepared primarily for the ice-cream trade, in large containers. Th
manufacturers can be persuaded to supply this direct to customers if their usual trad
outlets do not carry stocks. Substitute essence of almond for pistachio essence
necessary. If a food processor is not being used, whip the eggs whole with the sugar unt
frothy. Melt the butter and add it to the eggs and sugar with a few drops of essence. Fol
in the flour. Bake in a preheated oven on the middle shelf on gas mark 4 for 45 minute
Cool slightly and decant. Cut in half through the middle when cold.

For the filling and coating the sides of the gateaux whip *4 ozs of double cream* ar
add 1 oz icing sugar, 2 ozs coarsely ground pistachio nuts and 4 drops of pistach
essence. A further ounce of ground pistachio nuts should be used to cover the cream o
the sides of the gateaux.

For the iced topping use *3 ozs icing sugar, 4 drops of lemon juice, 4 drop
pistachio essence and 1 slighly beaten small egg white.* Make into a dough, roll in a circ
large enough to cover the top of the cake, and fix in position with a very *fine layer o
apricot jam* or golden syrup spread over the sponge.

Wedding Cake

Rich fruit cake, covered with marzipan and royal icing is made in many parts of the world for celebrations. In Calcutta and Bombay, in particular, the centrepiece of a Jewish wedding reception was an enormous rich fruit cake of up to five or six tiers, beautifully decorated with icing and silver trimmings. Curiously, this tradition does not appear to have come from Iraq and is more likely to have been influenced by and then elaborated from, the British Raj. The recipe is being included here because "wedding" cake came to be the most important refreshment on these occasions in the Indian Jewish community. Large portions were distributed the day following the wedding to close family members.

The quantities here will make a 4-5 lb cake. What distinguished the cakes made in India were the use of candied pumpkin, which I have seen here on sale sometimes before Christmas, and the generous use of spices such as cinnamon, nutmeg and ginger.

Beat 9 ozs of butter with *9 ozs brown sugar*. Add *5 eggs, one at a time*. Add the *rind and juice of 1 lemon, 3 tablespoons of brandy and 3 tablespoons of sherry. Sift 9 ozs of plain flour and mix with 2 teaspoons of ground cinnamon, 2 teaspoons of grated nutmeg and 1 teaspoon of powdered ginger*. Mix these powdered ingredients with *4 ozs of chopped glace cherries, 14 ozs of sultanas, 14 ozs raisins, 4 ozs blanched and chopped almonds and 7 ozs chopped mixed peel*. If candied pumpkin is available use this instead of the mixed peel. Add all this to the creamed mixture, folding thoroughly.

Pour into a 10" cake tin lined with greaseproof paper and take a double thickness newspaper and wrap it around the tin and secure with string. This will prevent the outside burning while the centre is raw. Bake on gas mark 1 for 5 hours, but longer if necessary. Leave to cool for 10 minutes in the tin and then turn out the cake on a wire rack until it is cold. Store in an air-tight container for at least a week, but longer if possible.

After a week at least, prepare the marzipan covering. Dissolve *12 ozs sugar* in *1 cup water* over medium heat. When it bubbles add *1 teaspoon of lemon juice.* Stir until the syrup makes fine threads when dropped from a spoon. This should take about 7 minutes. Lower the heat and add 6 ozs of finely ground almonds until the mixture is the consistency of soft dough. Add *3 more teaspoons of lemon juice, 1 capful of essence of vanilla and 1 capful of essence of almond.* Cool the mixture slightly and in the meantime *whisk 1 egg white*. Beat this in and cool the mixture completely, stirring from time to time.

Roll out the marzipan on a broad surface which has been liberally sprinkled with icing sugar to the thickness required. Cut out a round for the top and then a strip to go round the cake. Spread the top and sides of the fruit cake with a very light coat of *Golden Syrup*, or apricot jam to fix the marzipan. Smooth the edges. Store in an airtight container for at least another week when the cake may be iced.

Sift *12 ozs of icing sugar*. Whisk *2 egg whites* until very stiff. Add the icing sugar to the egg whites by folding in very gradually. Add *1 teaspoon lemon juice and 1 tablespoon rose water.* The rose water may be substituted with 1 teaspoon of essence of vanilla. Coat the marzipan with the icing mixture and smooth with a palette knife. When the icing is dry store in an airtight container until ready for use. Decorate as required.

Sweets

Gifts of a box of jewellery and a tray of baklawa, to sweeten the mouth, being delivered to a bride on the Sabbath eve before the wedding.

Sweets

Although the sweets here may be served after the main meal, many are at their best
ith a cup of after-dinner coffee, either instead of an elaborate dessert or after one. These
veets are generally eaten in small portions rather than in 'helpings', as traditionally most
them, particularly the range of loozenas, were served with a small cup of black coffee
henever friends happened to drop in or as a tea time treat.

Agar-Agar

This jelly is made from sea-weed sweetened and flavoured with rose water. Agar
ar can be bought at most Indian grocery shops, and looks rather like white straw. It also
mes in powdered form sold in individual packets by Japanese food shops.

It is very simple and quick to prepare. Dissolve *1 oz of agar agar* (in either the
aw or powdered form) in *2 $\frac{1}{2}$ pints of water.* Bring to the boil and simmer until the
aw-like substance or the powder is completely dissolved and add *5 ozs of sugar.* When
e sugar has dissolved turn off the heat and add $\frac{1}{2}$ *cup of rose water* and (optional but
ual) *a few drops of food colouring.*

Decant into individual pudding bowls or one large bowl, and cool. The traditonal
ay is to decant into a shallow, wide-bottomed dish and when cool, cut into diamond
apes and serve on a plate.

When the agar agar is cool, refrigerate and serve cold.

Coconut Agar Agar

This is made basically the same way as above except that a *7 oz. block of crea* *of coconut* should be dissolved in *2 ½ pints of water* when it is boiled with the agar ag. A layer of coconut cream will rise to the top.

Baba Khudrassi

This sweet resembles a small nougat cake. Boil *4 oz of sugar with 4 oz Gold* *Syrup, or sugar syrup,* until it forms into a ball when dropped into cold water. In t meantime whip the *white of a small egg* until it is very stiff. Turn the sugar off the he and allow the bubbles to settle. Then add the egg white, whisking briskly so that t mixture does not form into lumps. Add *4 oz of chopped pistachio nuts.*

Prepare a board generously dredged with flour. Drop one spoonful of the mixtu at a time on to the flour – leaving a little spreading space. Dredge the top of the ba khudrassi with flour.

When the mixture is cool enough to handle, work a little of the flour into the swe forming into the shape of a flattened ball.

The success of the sweet depends on getting the timing of cooking the sugar rig Under–cooking will mean the mixture will remain very soft and spread too much. Ove cooking will result in a very brittle texture.

Store with a generous spread of flour between each cake.

Baklawa

Baklawa, a rich almond and pastry sweet, is widely known throughout the Middle ast but methods of preparation vary from place to place. Traditionally, baklawa is ssociated with celebration, for example, gifts of jewellery from a bridegroom to a bride ould be sent with a dish of baklawa "to sweeten the mouth".

Start by making a dough with *1 1b self raising flour, 3 tablespoons vegetable il, ½ teaspoon salt and warm water to bind it.* Allow the pastry to rest for at least half n hour at room temperature. The texture should be soft but firm.

For the almond filling, grind *2 1bs of blanched almonds* – not too fine as the texture ould be crunchy. Add *6 ozs granulated sugar, 6 tablespoons of rosewater* (not essence f rosewater) and *crushed seeds from 8 to 10 cardimum pods.* The cardimum and the uantity of cardimum is optional.

A roasting tin 30 cm x 22 cm is just right to take this quantity of baklawa. Don't use non-stick tin if you can help it as the baklawa has to be cut with a sharp knife in the tray. repare the tray by brushing the bottom and sides with *½ tablespoon of vegetable oil.* ivide the pastry into 4 equal parts. Start by rolling out one part very thin and place in the ottom of the greased baking tray. Trim the sides. Divide the almond mixture into 3 equal arts. Spread one-third evenly over the bottom layer of pastry. Build up with alternate yers of pastry and almond mixture, brushing each successive layer of pastry ith *½ tablespoon of vegetable oil,* ending up with a layer of pastry, the top of which ould also be brushed with oil.

Using a sharp knife, cut through the layers of almond and pastry into diamond- aped pieces, pressing the pastry down as you go along to avoid crinkling the top layer. his should produce 30 or 35 pieces, depending on the size of each piece.

Bake in a preheated oven on the top shelf on gas mark 4 for 1 hour.

In the meantime prepare the syrup. Boil *1 cup of water* and add *10 ozs granulated ugar* which should be kept boiling on a low light for ten minutes. Let the baklawa cool little when it is removed from the oven and ladle the warm syrup over it evenly. Try to et the temperature of the baklawa and the syrup as even as possible.

When the baklawa is cold remove each piece separately and carefully. Store in an irtight container in a cool place and serve as required. Baklawa freezes very successfully.

Bread Pudding

Since milk products cannot be eaten immediately after a meal of meat or poultry coconut milk was often used as a substitute. Bread pudding is an example.

Place *4 oz cream of coconut* in *1 pint of boiling water.* Bring to the boil and simme until the coconut is thoroughly dissolved. Add *4 ozs of caster sugar.* When this too ha been dissolved add *1 capful essence of vanilla, 1 oz raisins and 1 oz of blanched almond cut into slivers.*

Turn off the heat and add 6 slices of stale white bread after trimming the crust Crush the bread into the liquid and bind with *1 beaten egg* until the mixture is fairl smooth and firm.

Turn into a pie dish and bake on the middle shelf in a preheated oven on gas mar 4, for one hour or until the top is golden brown.

Bread pudding may be served hot or cold. It stores well for a few days covered i the refrigerator.

Cornflour Pudding

This pudding is derived from the Middle East but has been adapted by the India Jewish community substituting coconut milk or citrus fruit juice for cow's milk.

Dissolve $\frac{1}{2}$ *cake of cream of coconut* and *5 ozs of sugar in 1 pint of water.* Brir this to the boil and then simmer until the coconut cream and the sugar dissolves. In separate bowl dissolve *4 ozs of cornflour in* $\frac{1}{2}$ *pint of cold water.* Add this graduall to the sugar and coconut water, stirring constantly over a low flame until the mixtu thickens. Turn off the heat, add a few drops of food colouring (optional) and *1 capful essence of vanilla.* Turn out into a shallow serving dish and as the mixture cools sprink the top with *2 oz of blanched almonds* cut into slivers.

Traditionally cornflour pudding is cut into diamond shapes and served i individual pieces.

Coconut water does not appear to be used very much in the Middle East and for th particular pudding citrus fruit juice might be used. This makes a light and refreshin pudding and is particularly delicious if fresh or canned citrus fruit is added to the cornflo mixture. Decorate with fruit and / or slivered almonds and sprinkle with cinnamo powder.

Dodail

The ingredients used in Dodail suggest an Indian influence. Dissolve *4 oz of coconut cream in 1 pint of water.* Add *1 cup of ground rice* and for authenticity add cup of jaggery available in Indian grocery shops. This is a sugar substitute but has a very distinctive flavour. Sometimes halek or date juice is used instead of jaggery and this too delicious. If these ingredients are not available then use brown sugar.

Mix the ingredients together and stir on a high flame which should be reduced very low as the dodail begins to thicken. When the mixture has thickened turn off the heat and add either *1 cap of essence of vanilla or 1 tablespoon of rosewater.* A few ground cardimum seeds is an optional extra flavouring.

Decant into a shallow dish and sprinkle the top with slivered almonds.
Serve cold.

Hulkoon (Turkish Delight)

This sweet was not usually made in individual homes but by Jewish confectioners.
Dissolve *2 lbs of sugar in $\frac{1}{4}$ pint of water* by bringing to the boil in a preserving an. Then simmer, stirring occasionally. In a separate bowl mix *3 oz of cornflour in nough cold water* to produce a smooth paste and gradually increase the water to *$\frac{3}{4}$ of pint.* Pour the syrup into the cornflour very gradually, stirring all the time until the mixture is quite smooth. Transfer back into the preserving pan, bring to the boil and mmer. Stir from time to time. When the back of a spoon can be coated with the mixture s it thickens remove from the heat. It requires experience to judge the cooking time. It takes at least $1\frac{1}{2}$ hours on simmer, with occasional stirring, to reach this point. Under-cooking can result in a "stringy" consistency whilst overcooking can crystallise the mixture.

When the liquid is removed from the heat add the flavourings. This can be varied y pouring the hot liquid into different vessels. *Rose water* is a great favourite. Add *3 to tablespoons, a few drops of red food colouring and scatter 1 oz of pistachio nuts* into he mixture. For a lemon flavouring add the *juice of lemon, a few drops of yellow food olouring and an ounce of pistachio nuts.* For orange flavouring add the *juice of 1 range, a few drops of orange food colouring and an ounce of pistachio nuts.*

Stir and decant into shallow trays which have been dusted with *a mixture of ornflour and icing sugar.* Smooth the surface, and leave to set. When cold cut into small quares and roll each one in a mixture of cornflour and icing sugar.

Store in an airtight container, and sprinkle each layer liberally with cornflour and cing sugar.

Hulwarashi

What we call Hulwarashi is made widely in the Middle East and is known simp' as hulwa, or sometimes Israeli hulwa, since it is exported from there. It is very quick ar easy to make at home.

Bake *1 cup of sesame seeds* until slightly toasted or just golden and when cool grir to a powder.

Dissolve $\frac{3}{4}$ *of a cup of sugar in 1 cup of warm water.* Simmer. Heat *4 tablespoon of vegetable oil* and add the powdered sesame seeds. Keep stirring over a low light f' five to ten minutes until the aroma rises. Remove from the heat and add, very graduall the sugar water. Care should be taken as the mixture tends to splash slightly at first. Ac *1 capful of essence of vanilla* and *half a cup of chopped pistachio nuts.*

Turn out on to a greased surface in the shape of a compact block.

When cold, store in an air-tight container. Cut off slices as required.

Kamroodeen

This is an apricot based sweet, which originated from the Middle East.
Soak *2 lbs of dried apricots* so that the water level is a little higher than that of the aprico' Let it stand overnight and then liquidise. Use a preserving pan if possible to boil *1 lb* sugar in 6 tablespoons of water.* (The sugar can be adjusted to taste).

As the sugar and water bubbles add the *juice of half a lemon.* Stir until the sug coats the back of a metal spoon. Add the liquidised apricots and boil. Turn down the he until the mixture just stays bubbling.

Continue cooking to reduce the mixture. First it will thicken and eventually be a heavy paste-like consistency. When the mixture leaves the sides of the pan it is reac to set. This could take about two hours, during which time regular stirring is necessar Towards the end of the cooking time the colour of the apricots will darken.

When ready to set either pour into a shallow dish or in a thin layer on bakir parchment. When it begins to cool place another layer of baking parchment on the surfa' and go over it with a rolling pin. This will produce an even thickness and smooth surfac The top layer of baking parchment may then be removed and should peel away qui easily.

Leave to dry out for several hours at room temperature. The Kamroodeen set c baking parchment may be rolled (with the paper) and stored in an airtight container. If is in a dish, cut into diamond shapes and dust lightly with icing sugar. Store in a steri jar in a cool place. Kamroodeen has a long shelf life if properly stored.

Aamsath

This is a mango-based sweet which is very similar to kamroodeen.

Kamroodeen is widely known in the Middle East while aamsath is from India, but e method of preparation is the same and only the basic ingredient is different. It is likely at the culinary traditions of the Middle East were carried further east first by the Moghul nquest of Northern India, and reinforced by the Jews on a much smaller scale.

Use *2 large tins (30 oz size) of mango pulp.* Alphonso mangoes are best. Since the nned pulp is sweetened, use *12 oz of sugar* instead of 1 1b recommended for apricots.

Almond Loozena

"Loozena" means diamond shaped, and many sweets are presented in this way.

Dissolve *6 oz sugar in 6 tablespoons of water* by bringing to the boil and simmering r five to ten minutes, by which time the sugar will form into threads. Add *2 tablespoons f rose water* and continue to simmer for a couple of minutes. Then add *8 ozs coarsely round almonds, 1 dessertspoon of cinnamon powder and ground cardimum seeds ptional).* Mix thoroughly and continue to cook until the mixture leaves the sides of the n.

Pour on to a baking sheet in the shape of a square or oblong. Place another sheet baking paper over the mixture and go over with a rolling pin to get a smooth surface. emove the top sheet of baking paper and as the mixture begins to cool, cut into diamond apes. Start by making the longest diagonal cut and then continue cutting on either side fairly narrow strips. Use a sharp knife dipped in boiling water to prevent the paste from icking. Alternatively, wait till the mixture is cold before cutting. The loozenas should about half an inch thick. When cold separate the loozenas and store in an air-tight ntainer.

Serve with coffee.

For those who can get rose water syrup there is an even quicker and easier way make almond loozena. Mix the *sugar, ground almounds and cinnamon.* Warm *tablespoons of water* in a pan and add the dry ingredients. Mix and stir well over a very w flame. Then add *2 tablespoons of rose water syrup.* This is usually tinged with pink plouring and is available in many Indian grocery shops. Stir gently until the mixture is f a sticky consistency then turn out and cut into diamond shapes as suggested above.

Coconut Loozena

Moisten, but do not soak, *7 oz of coarse dessicated coconut* in enough *cold water* resemble the consistency of a freshly grated coconut (about *2 tablespoons*).

Dissolve *1 cup of sugar in 3 tablespoons of hot water*. Bring to the boil and simmer f five to ten minutes when the sugar should form threads. Add the coconut and s constantly until the mixture leaves the sides of the pan. Turn off the heat and add *1 capful essence of vanilla (or to taste), a few ground cardimum seeds* (optional) and *a few drops food colouring* (also optional). Flavouring with cardimum seeds is very popular with t Iraqi-Indian community but this could be an acquired taste.

Turn out the mixture onto a sheet of baking paper and flatten the surface with broad-bladed knife until it is ½″ thick. When the mixture cools slightly cut into diamo shapes. Separate the pieces when they are quite cold.

Store in an air tight container in a cool place.

Serve with black coffee as an after-dinner treat.

Guava Loozena and Guava Jelly

These two delicacies can be made at the same time with fresh ripe guavas. Choose ɹavas which have just turned yellow. These are in season in winter.

Wash and cut into small pieces *3 lbs of guavas.* No need to peel the outer skin or ɩmove the seeds. Cover with *3 pints of cold water* and boil until the guavas are of a pulp-ɕe consistency.

Place the softened guavas in a cheese cloth and leave to hang over a preserving pan ∕ernight to accumulate the dripping liquid. Do not squeeze or else the jelly will be cloudy ther than clear.

ɔ make the jelly :

Add *1 lb of sugar to each pint of the liquid.* Boil and then simmer until setting point reached (220°F, 105°C). Pour the jelly into warm, sterilised jars and cover the tops with axed paper. The jelly should have an indefinite shelf life if stored in a cool place.

ɔ make the loozena :

Sieve the guava flesh to separate it from the seeds which should be discarded. Add *lb of sugar to every pound of guava pulp.* Boil in a preserving pan, and then reduce the ɕat until the pulp just simmers. Stir from time to time and continue cooking until the ɹava pulp is of a paste-like consistency and leaves the sides of the pan. This could take least $1\frac{1}{2}$ hours, and the pulp needs to be stirred from time to time.

When setting point is reached, pour into a shallow dish to cool. Dust lightly with ɩng sugar or ground almonds, cut into diamond shapes, and store in an air-tight ɔntainer.

Exactly the same method may be used to make *QUINCE LOOZENA AND ELLY.* Substitute the quince for the guava.

Hazelnut and Chocolate Loozena

This is not a traditional recipe for loozena but is included here to encourage reader to use a variety of ingredients and apply methods which are basic to our style of cooking

Roast *8 ozs of ground hazelnuts* in the oven or in a dry pan until the aroma rise Set aside. Dissolve *4 ozs of sugar* in $\frac{1}{4}$ *pint of water,* bring to the boil, stir from time time and simmer for seven to ten minutes. Meanwhile melt *4 ozs of cooking chocola* preferably by using a double saucepan, and add this to the syrup stirring all the time. the syrup becomes almost entirely absorbed add *a tablespoon or two of water* and s till smooth. Add the hazelnuts and continue to stir over a low flame until the mixtu leaves the sides of the pan.

Decant on baking paper on a tray. Place another sheet of baking paper on the surfa and go over it with a rolling pin. The mixture should be approximately half an inch dee

When the mixture is cool strip off the top sheet of baking paper and cut into looze shapes.

When cold, store in an air-tight container.

Orange Loozena

According to Daisy Iny, Orange Loozena was part of the repertoire of Baghdadi ooking. This was not continued in India as oranges grown in the Middle East were not vailable there. What we called oranges are known as tangerines in the Western world. owever, now that Middle East oranges are widely exported, orange loozena can fit in gain into this range of sweets. The Baghdadi method described by Mrs Iny is fairly borious and I suggest a simpler way, using the method basic to other loozenas.

Use a zester or grater to strip the *rind of 2 oranges.* Squeeze the *juice of the 2 ranges,* add the rind and *6 ozs of sugar.* Bring this to the boil, stirring from time to time, d then simmer until the juice forms threads. This should take about seven to ten minutes. dd *8 ozs of coarsely ground almonds* and continue to cook on a very low light until the ixture leaves the sides of the pan.

Place a sheet of baking paper on a tray and decant. Place another sheet of baking per on the surface and go over with a rolling pin to get a smooth surface. The mixture ould be about half an inch thick.

When cool, strip off the baking paper and cut into loozena shapes and store in an r-tight container when cold.

Suggested variations are to substitute lemons for oranges, and the juice of half a mon may be diluted with the required quantity of water so that it is not too sharp. Ground monds may be subtituted by ground walnuts, and this would blend well with orange.

Pistachio Loozena

Buy unsalted, shelled pistachio nuts and grind coarsely. For *8 oz of pistachio* nuts ou will need *6 ozs of sugar. Dissolve the sugar in 6 tablespoons of water* by bringing the boil and then simmering for five to ten minutes, by which time the sugar will form to threads. Add the pistachio nuts and mix throughly until the mixture leaves the sides the pan.

Pour out on to a baking sheet in the shape of a square or oblong. Place another sheet baking paper over the mixture and go over with a rolling pin to get a smooth surface. en remove the top sheet of baking paper. As the mixture begins to cool, cut into amond shapes. The loozenas should be about half an inch thick. When quite cold, parate the loozenas and store in an air-tight container. If stored in a cool place the ozenas will have a long shelf life - several weeks at least.

The loozenas may be dusted with icing sugar but this is not essential. Some people efer to spread silver leaf. This is typically Indian and adds a festive touch.

Pumpkin Loozena

Buy a pumpkin suitable for preserving or making "maraba". This should be ha
and fleshy, but may not be very easily obtainable in Indian grocery shops, in which ca
the white variety, with a very pale green skin may be substituted. It is not ideal but I ha
used it successfully.

Grate the flesh of the pumpkin coarsely, parboil and drain.

For each *pound weight of pumpkin* (weighed after it has been peeled and the se
pods removed) **use** *12 ozs of sugar.* Dissolve the sugar in just enough water to moist
it. Bring to the boil and simmer for about ten minutes, when the sugar should form threac

Add the grated pumpkin to the sugar and bring to the boil. The water content w
then increase as it exudes from the pumpkin. Allow the pumpkin to cook on simmer
the syrup until all the syrup has been absorbed and the pumpkin leaves the sides of the pa
This could take about an hour but would depend on the water content of the pumpkin use
Stir from time to time, particularly when the syrup is being absorbed towards the end
the cooking.

When the pumpkin has reached setting point and all the syrup has been absorbe
flavour with *ground cardimum seeds* and for *each pound of pumpkin* add *1 tablespo*
of rose water. Mix thoroughly before turning out on to a tray dredged with *sifted ici*
sugar and ground almonds. The exact quantity will depend on the amount cooked, t
for the quantities suggested here you will need *2 ozs each of icing sugar and grou*
almonds.

Flatten the pumpkin until it is about a quarter of an inch thick, making sure t
pieces are packed together. Dredge the surface with a mixture of icing sugar and grou
almonds.

When the mixture is cool, cut into diamond or loozena shapes.

Allow the loozenas to dry out at room temperature for a couple of days. Turn the
about twice a day. When they have dried out store in an airtight container.

This is a very fine sweet. Although the flavouring with cardimum seeds and ro
water is traditional, this can be omitted.

Mango maraba (Preserve)

This is a sharp preserve as it is made with green cooking mangoes. Select fleshy nes to ensure that substance remains in the mangoes after approximately 45 minutes of oking. Mango preserve is a good example of adapting Indian ingredients to a Middle istern style of cooking.

Weigh the *mangoes* and set aside. Then measure *an equal weight of sugar.* Place ie sugar in a preserving pan and dissolve in *enough water to cover the mangoes* when icy are to be added. Boil the sugar and water and simmer for 10 minutes. In the meantime cel the mangoes, discard the seed from the centre and add to the simmering syrup)gether with *a few cloves* and *a little lemon juice - say 1 teaspoon to each pound of iangoes.* Bring this to the boil and simmer until the mangoes become glazed and the yrup has reached setting point. This can be tested by placing a spoon of syrup on a cold late and waiting a few minutes to see whether the syrup has jelled or thickened. If some f the mangoes break up slightly in the cooking and become integrated with the syrup this s all to the good as the syrup will become enriched. Remove the froth from the sugar as t cooks.

When the maraba is cold, decant into cold jars. The mangoes should be covered vith syrup to ensure a long shelf life.

The traditional way to eat this maraba is as a sweet with black coffee, but it can be pread on buttered bread, toast or scones.

Mango Sorbet

Separate *3 eggs*. Add *3 tablespoons of caster sugar* to the yolks and cream togeth
with *1 teaspoon of sunflower oil*. Take *a large tin of mango pulp* (preferably Alphon
mango) or the flesh of 6 mangoes and blend with the egg yolk mixture.

Whip the egg whites until stiff and fold in the yolk mixture.

Freeze for 2 hours. Remove from freezer, churn and refreeze.

Store in plastic boxes in the freezer and use as necessary.

Peach Maraba (Preserve)

This preserve was made in Baghadad, according to Daisy Iny, but the preparatic
is different.

Buy backward peaches for maraba. Wash them thoroughly and dry the skins
ensure the maraba will not mould later.

Weigh the *fruit* and then weigh an *equal quantity of sugar.* Dissolve the sug
in water which will be sufficient to cover the fruit when it is cooked - the fruit level shou
be just under the level of the syrup, not floating in it. Boil the water and sugar and simm
for ten minutes. Add *a few cloves* and the fruit. Again bring it to the boil and simm
until the skins of the fruit become quite glazed and the syrup coats the back of a spoo

Decant and bottle when it is cold into cold jars.

Petar

This delicacy from Cochin is made from a filling of coconut and sugar and encased a pancake.

For the filling, grate *8 ozs of fresh coconut* or use dessicated coconut and mix th just enough water to mosten it and combine this with *8 ozs of sugar*. A *few cardimum eds* may be ground and added for extra flavour. Set aside.

Make the pancakes by mixing *1 cup of plain flour with 1 small egg, $1\frac{1}{2}$ cups of coconut milk, 2 teaspoons of sugar* and a *small pinch of salt*. The coconut milk may bought in cans or $3\frac{1}{2}$ ozs of cream of coconut can be dissolved in $1\frac{1}{2}$ cups of water. llow the mixture to stand for about half an hour, preferably in the refrigerator.

Grease the bottom of a 6" frying pan until it is very hot. Reduce the heat and add tablespoons of the pancake mixture. Lift as soon as the edges cook, turn and cook for other minute.

When the pancake has cooled, take a heaped tablespoon of the filling and place it 1 one side of the pancake. Cover with the other side and seal with a little of the pancake ixture.

Dissolve *half a cup of jaggery* in *half a cup of warm water*. Brown sugar may be ed as a substitute if necessary. Bring this to the boil and cool. Pour a tablespoon of the rup over the pancake.

This will make an unusual after dinner sweet although in Cochin it was a tea time at.

Pistachio Ice Cream

Bring *2 tins of evaporated milk (14 ozs)* to the boil. Simmer for 20 minutes. efrigerate overnight.

The next day whip the milk and add *1 tin sweetened condensed milk (14 oz,)7 gr) 1 teaspoon sunflower oil, 4 tablespoons caster sugar, 1 teaspoon pistachio or 'mond essence and a few drops of green food colouring (optional)*. Fold in *6 oz shelled 1d ground pistachio nuts of a crunchy consistency.*

Freeze in a covered plastic container.

After 2 hours remove from the freezer, churn and refreeze. Repeat the churning rocess at least once more.

Freeze and store until ready for use.

*Puah**

Puah is virtually a batter made of *8 oz plain flour (preferably wholemeal), 4 o₂ caster sugar, with enough water to make a heavy batter.*

About 1 tablespoon at a time should be dropped around a pan of boiling *vegetable o₁ sunflower oil,* and deep fried to a golden brown colour. This is plain puah.

For banana puah cut ripe bananas into wedges and drop them into the puah batter coat and deep fry.

These are the traditional ways but I have a suggestion for apple puah. Take *2 larg₂ Bramley apples, peel and cut into mouth sized pieces.* Sprinkle with *1 teaspoon ₀ cinnamon powder, $\frac{1}{2}$ teaspoon of nutmeg and 2 tablespoons of brown sugar.* Let th₂ apples rest until moist and drain off the liquid into the batter.

Drop the apple pieces into the puah batter, coat and deep fry until golden brown Puahs are best when eaten immediately after they are fried. All the preparation can b₂ done beforehand, leaving the frying until just before serving.

*   In Bombay this is called Malpuah.

Pumpkin Maraba (Preserve)

Preserving fruit and vegetables is comon practice throughout the Middle East and sewhere but crystallised pumpkin is an Indian speciality which can be bought in markets id from street vendors in most large cities in Northern India. Pumpkin preserve is a fine id popular variation of crystallised pumpkin.

In order to make this preserve successfully it is necessary to have the right type of impkin. Ask your Indian greengrocer for a pumpkin suitable for making jam or iaraba' rather than the varieties suitable for curry or bhaji. This should be hard and :shy with a low water content. Unfortunately this variety is highly perishable and is not great demand so that imports are scarce. It may not be particularly helpful to know the ime of this variety of pumpkin because it differs from province to province. Bengalis ill it "Chulkomo", and the Gujeratis say "Kora". It might be simpler to explain your irpose for you can be sure that the shop-keeper will be ready to assist as much as)ssible.

I have made the preserve with pumpkin usually used in bhajis with partial success. he taste is not at all different from the authentic maraba but the consistency is different. should be crunchy on the outside, soft inside, and plump enough to sink your teeth into . The result from the pale green pumpkin resembles the peel more than the flesh of the :getable. For those prepared to sacrifice consistency and settle for taste, the pale green impkin - commonly known as "sada kudoo" or white pumpkin, will do.

Peel the pumpkin(s), cut in half and dispose of the seeds and seed pods. Then weigh ie vegetable. Cut into wedges, approximately 3" x 4" and set aside.

Weigh the amount of *sugar* which is equivalent to the *weight of the pumpkin* and Id just enough water to moisten the sugar. Bring this to the boil and simmer for about n minutes. Add *a few cardimum seeds* to the sugar for additional flavour but this is ptional. Then add *a teaspoon of lemon juice* to every pound of sugar, stir and put the impkin pieces into the syrup. Bring to the boil and then simmer over a very low flame ntil the pumpkin becomes glazed. This could take at least an hour, particularly if the pale reen pumpkin is used as it has a high water content. When the syrup thickens sufficiently) coat the back of a spoon, remove from the heat and for each pound of sugar add *1 iblespoon of rose water.* Stir gently.

When the fruit and syrup become cold decant into cold jars and store in a cool place. here should be sufficient syrup to cover the pumpkin to ensure a long shelf life.

Serve with black coffee.

Simsimee

These are sesame cakes. Dissolve *4 oz sugar and 4 oz jaggery* (obtainable from most Indian grocery shops). If this is not convenient use honey or sugar syrup, sold here as Golden Syrup, very gradually over a low flame. When the sugar and jaggery caramalise add *8 oz of sesame seeds* which have been slightly toasted.

A spoonful of the mixture should be placed on a baking sheet and then moulded into a small dome shape. Repeat until the mixture has been entirely used in this way.

Foods for Festivals

Silver ware for the celebration of festivals and the
Sabbath. Left. "Koom-koom" rose water sprinkled from
the top of the vessel offered to guests on festivals.
Right: "Kiddush" cup for benediction over wine on the
Sabbath and festivals.

Foods for Festivals

The Jewish calendar, like others is punctuated by a series of festivals and fasts. It
s worth saying something about these special days because they are so important in the
fe of Jewish communities throughout the world, and on which many customs and
aditions have come to be built.

Before talking about festivals it is appropriate to emphasise the place of the sabbath
ay in Jewish life because it is the special day in the week. The religious commandment
a Exodus 20:8, "Six days shall you labour ... but the seventh day is a sabbath ... in it you
hall do no manner of work" is repeated time and again to underline its importance. This
ay of rest has come to be significant in the Judaeo-Christian tradition and as such it has
ad world-wide impact. The sabbath day is to be observed by the entire household,
ncluding servants, "the stranger that is within your gates" and extended to working
nimals. From this basis an entire structure of social customs and practice has evolved.
ositive ways and means of enjoying the day were developed to set it apart from the rest
f the week such as lighting lamps or candles, reciting benedictions over wine and bread,
nging special songs and eating three substantial meals. The first meal is when Sabbath
omes in on Friday night and the entire family usually gather together, the last meal is
aten just before Sabbath goes out, and there is one meal in between, at lunch time. Some
f the favourite foods prepared for the sabbath day by the Iraqi-Indian commmunity have
lready been singled out.

In Judaism, as in most other cultures, food has always been a special and social way
» emphasise the importance of the "good days" - the sabbath and festivals. Eating the
ost substantial meals, the tastiest dishes, the most delicate sweets, is a means of
hannelling religious ideas into feelings and hopefully to appropriate action. This will be
llustrated in the following pages where the origins and some customs of the festivals will
e discussed together with recipes for foods which were traditionally prepared in the
ommunity.

Jewish law and practice have been handed down in two ways - the Written Law and
ne Oral Law, and both have a role in instruction. For example, we praise God for the food
e eat as a form of religious etiquette. There seems to be a contradiction between two
iblical verses in this context. First, "the earth is the Lord's and the fulness thereof; the
orld and they that dwell therein" Psalms 24:1 that is, everything on earth belongs to God
xclusively. However, Psalm 115:16 "The heavens are the heavens of the Lord, but the
arth He has given to the children of men" is a statement that the material is for mankind.
he rabbis resolve the anomaly by pointing to Deuteronomy 8:10 "You shall eat and be
atisfied and bless the Lord for the good land which He has given you". We may eat and
e satisfied but we must remember to thank God for it.

The Oral Law is bound up with tradition, and part of the tradition involves eating
pecific foods. These have a number of functions, symbolising events, acting as

reminders of moral issues, and embodying our worthy hopes and aspirations. This wi
be seen, to some extent, from what follows in this section. However, traditional foods f
particular festive seasons vary between communities and some foods which are eate
traditionally at public and private celebrations are not at all symbolic and represent r
more than the richest or most popular dishes known within a community.

The Jewish year is based on the lunar calendar so there is always some variatic
from the solar calendar which is generally used. The New Year or Rosh Hashana is son
time in September or October. Although it is a feast there is a sombre note too becau
it ushers a penetential period which culminates ten days later in a fast on the Day
Atonement. For it says in Leviticus 23:11 "You shall afflict your souls ... to mal
atonement... it is a statute throughout your generations in all your dwellings".

When my grandfather returned from the synagogue after the Day of Atonement, tl
first thing he did, even before breaking his fast, was to place palm leaves on the "succ
or temporary structure in which we ate our meals during the week of the Festival
Tabernacles which follows five days after the Day of Atonement. This symbolises the el
of a period of introspection and a movement towards a time for pleasure which requir
an emotional development. Although the festival of Tabernacles is a time for celebratic
our joy is tempered with a reminder of our own frailty and impermanence, represente
by the temporary structures we build and use for these days. Immediately following tl
feast is Simhat Torah or Rejoicing of the Law. It is a time for unmitigated joy, celebrat
with song and good food in the home and with song and dance in the synagogue. Tl
Scrolls of the Law are taken out from the Ark and displayed outside it. In Calcutta tl
synagogue was draped from end to end with richly embroidered cloths of silk and velv
in deep colours and the setting was magnificent. A fit setting, in fact, to complete tl
reading from Deuteronomy, the last of the Five Books of Moses, and to commen
immediately the reading from the first chapter of Genesis, the first of the Five Book
signifying that there is no end to the cycle of learning.

Next comes Channukah, a minor festival of post-Biblical origin. This is
commemorate a miracle at the time of the rededication of the Temple, when oil sufficic
for lighting on only one night lasted for eight nights. We light candles or lamps each nig
adding an extra one as we go through the week. Channukah comes in mid-wint
coinciding roughly with Christmas and this may be the reason why it is highlighted in t
West, with gifts for the children. Gift giving was not a custom in my own communit

Channukah is followed by Purim in early spring and this is also a minor festiv
As it says in the Book of Esther 9:24 we mark out this day in the year because "Hamar
the enemy of all the Jews had devised against the Jews to destroy them, and had cast p
that is, the lot, to discomfit them and to destroy them... wherefore they called these da
Purim, after the name of pur". It was through the personal intervention of Queen Estl
who risked her own life and saved the lives of her people that the "Jews had rest from th
enemies ... when sorrow turned to gladness and mourning into a good day; that they shot
make days of feasting and gladness, and of sending portions one to another and gifts
the poor". Esther, 9:22.

One month after Purim is the festival of Passover, when we celebrate freedom from slavery and recall the events which led up to this deliverance. The word Passover comes from Exodus 12:13, 17 "... I (God) shall pass over you (the Hebrews) and there shall be no plague upon you to destroy you when I smite the land of Egypt. And this day shall be to you a memorial and you shall keep it a feast to the Lord; throughout your generations . it is a feast by an ordinance for ever". "Seven days shall you eat unleavened bread, ... or in this selfsame day have I brought your hosts out of the land of Egypt".

Shavuoth, or the Festival of Weeks usually coincides with Pentecost and is sometimes called by that name. The festival is called "Weeks" because it says in Deuteronomy 16:10, 11 "Seven weeks shall you number ... from the time the sickle is first put to the standing corn you shall begin to number seven weeks and you shall keep the feast of Weeks unto the Lord...and rejoice". Traditionally forty-nine days are counted from the second night of Passover until the night before Shavouth. The agricultural importance of the festival is clear from the above, but verse 12 of the same chapter contains the elements of the second reason for this festival. "And you shall remember that you were a slave in Egypt and you shall observe and do these statutes". There is a clear imperative for individual moral responsibility, for it is not merely that the Hebrews were literally enslaved by the Egyptians and had to learn to merit their freedom. Every individual is enslaved by inclinations to look to their own interests until, through a process of understanding and education, accept that liberty is achieved through responsibility for ourselves and for the community in which we live. The communal acceptance of such responsibility is described in a scene in Deuteronomy 24:3 "And Moses came and told the people all the words of the Lord, and all the ordinances; and all the people answered with one voice and said 'All the words which the Lord has spoken will we do' ".

There may be unity in the heritage of Judaism concerning its basic framework, but there is considerable diversity in many practical ways, particularly as they relate to the cultural differences between communities in various parts of the world. The dispersion of the Jews for some 2000 years has ensured this diversity. Sometimes the differences, expressed in music, art and cooking are so great as to be scarcely recognisable from one community to another. However, we now live in an age when it is possible to collect and document information on our diversity and this knowledge can only extend our horizons and enrich our individual experience.

Cooking "matza" or unleavened bread in the compound of one of the Calcutta synagogues, in makeshift kitchens, just before Passover.

"atzoth" would be collected and stored
large baskets lined with cloth and
spended from the ceiling for protection from vermin

On the eve of the Jewish New Year, Rosh Hashana, we have a ritual celebration round the dinner table. After the traditional blessings on wine and bread Sephardi Jews precede the meal by eating a selection of foods which are symbolic. For example, we eat figs or pomegranate because these fruits have numerous seeds and we do so with the prayer that our good deeds in the coming year may match the number of seeds in the particular fruit. Both Sephardi and Ashkenazi Jews usually eat apple dipped in honey or sugar on this night. We give thanks to God who "creates the fruit of trees" and pray that it will be His will "to grant us a year from the first day to the last, as goodly as the apple and as sweet as honey".

This is the way we prepare the apple delicacy which is virtually an apple preserve. I prefer a sharp eating apple, such as Granny Smiths or Worcester, but others may prefer a sweet apple. What matters is that an eating rather than a cooking apple should be used.

Peel and core the apples and for each *pound of fruit use a pound of sugar.* For each pound of apples use $\frac{1}{2}$ *pint of cold water,* $\frac{1}{2}$ *teaspoon of fresh lemon juice, 2 cloves or cardimum pods and 1 tablespoon of rose water.* Dissolve the sugar in the water by bringing to the boil and simmering for ten minutes. Add the lemon juice, cloves, cardimum and the apples. Bring to the boil and then simmer until the apples are glazed. This could take approximately an hour. Setting point will have been reached when the syrup coats the back of a spoon, and the apples and syrup become tinged with a glowing colour. Remove from the heat and add the rose water. This should be done gently to avoid breaking up the fruit. When cold, decant into a cold jar or container. The preserve will have a long shelf life and may be used as jam.

The Festival of Tabernacles coincides with the fruit harvest in Israel. We build a "succa" or temporary structure for this festival and it is customary to eat all our meals there. Leviticus 24:42:43 says "You shall dwell in booths seven days ... that your generations may know that I made the children of Israel to dwell in booths when I brought them out of the land of Egypt." The booths are covered with leaves and decorated with fruit since it says in Leviticus 23:40 "And you shall take... the fruit of goodly trees, palm trees and boughs of thick trees and willows of the brook, and you shall rejoice before the Lord... seven days". Not only did we adorn the "succa" with fruit, we also had fairy lights, glass balls in a variety of sizes and colours and decorations made from coloured foil. The fruit we hung up was usually backward at the start of the festival so that we could gradually eat it as it ripened in the week that followed. We used whatever fruit was in season, bananas, apples, oranges, custard apples and "safeyda" and "amra" which are now being imported here.

Traditionally, another festival treat is roasted nuts and these were offered to guests who called to share in the celebrations.

FISTAK or pistachio nuts. These are prepared by washing the nuts, sometime shelled, but more often in their shells, draining them and transferring into a pan an roasting over an open fire. It is just as efficient and certainly less time consuming to us the oven. Sprinkle the nuts with salt - the amount will depend on taste - but approximatel *one or two tablespoons to a pound of nuts* should be sufficient. Bake in a preheated ove on gas mark 6 (middle shelf) for 20 to 30 minutes. When cold store in an air-tigh container.

BINDAK or almonds. Wash and drain the almonds. Sprinkle with salt as suggeste above and bake for 15 to 20 minutes in a preheated oven on gas mark 6 (middle shelf The skins are left on the almonds. When cold store in an airtight container.

FINDAK or hazelnuts are not salted but roasted or toasted with the skins for 15 2 20 minutes in a preheated oven gas mark 6 (middle shelf). Store in an air-tight contain when cold.

CHURGOSA or pine nuts are washed and roasted in their shells without sal Twenty minutes should be sufficient roasting time in a preheated oven 'gas mark ((middle shelf). Store in an airtight container when cold.

Simhat Torah or the Festival of Rejoicing of the Law is celebrated immediate after the Festival of Tabernacles. Congregations move in procession seven times rour the synagogue, carrying the Scrolls of the Law in turn, accompanied by singing ar dancing.

In most homes, at least part of the celebration would mean eating a sumptuous me of roast chicken, aloomakalla, khutta and pilaw. Many families would prepare pilaw a special way on this occasion. It would contain an additional ingredient calle SHA'AREE. This is prepared two evenings before it is used. Sha'aree is made from *whi flour, a little salt and enough cold water to bind it.* The dough is covered and left to stai for at least an hour. Then a tiny piece is pinched out and rolled once or twice between tl forefinger and thumb and dropped on to a tray until all the dough is used. It is then le uncovered - well spread out on a tray - to dry out at room temperature.

Sha'aree is a form of pasta and resembles a large grain of rice. It is now availab from Greek and Israeli greengroceries.

When the pilaw is to be cooked, deep fry the Sha'aree in vegetable oil until it golden brown. It is mixed with the rice in the preparation of pilaw (see above) just befo the water is added.

The end result is a mixture of yellow rice with golden brown Sha'aree - which very colourful.

Chunukah is a festival which celebrates the rededication of the Temple and the miracle of the oil which burned the sacred lamp for eight nights when it seemed sufficient for one night only. It is a time when we eat HALWA as it is both sweet and is cooked in oil. Halwa resembles a soft but firm semolina cake.

Dissolve $\frac{3}{4}$ *of a cup of caster sugar in 1 cup of warm water* and set aside. Blanch *oz of almonds cut in slivers* and set aside. Stir *1 cup of semolina in half a cup of vegetable oil* over medium heat for 10 minutes or until the semolina is a golden colour and is thoroughly cooked. Remove from the heat and add the dissolved sugar water, the almonds and *1 oz of raisins.* Mix thoroughly over low heat for a couple of minutes. Turn off the heat and add *half a cup of rosewater* or a *capful of essence of vanilla.*

Turn into a one-pint pudding bowl. When cool ease the semolina cake from the sides of the bowl, turn out on to a dish and serve cold.

Halwa may be eaten as a sweet but it is quite common to spread it on bread or eat with fried Indian bread such as purees or paratas.

The festival of Purim celebrates the redemption of the Jews from the hands of Haman, chief minister to King Ahasuerus of Persia who planned to exterminate them, and is recorded in the Book of Esther. This was achieved through the personal and heroic intervention of Queen Esther. The Jews "stood for their lives and had rest from their enemies ... therefore (it is) a day of gladness and feasting, and a good day, and of sending portions one to another". Esther 9:13 and 19.

The "sending of portions" is a custom widely preserved by exchanging gifts of sweets, cakes and delicacies. All the foods listed in the section on "Baked Goodies" are still generally used and especially the variety of loozenas and baklava in the section on "Sweets".

The eve of Passover is a time for families to get together in their homes and celebrate by going over the story of the Exodus from Egypt. We recall the enslavement and in doing so appreciate even more the liberation and freedom which follows. We recall, amongst other events, that the Hebrews built cities in Egypt whilst in slavery and a food called "haroseth" symbolises the bricks and mortar made for this purpose. The ingredients used to make "haroseth" vary between communities and in our tradition it is known as HALEK, which is cooked date juice. It is a delicious preparation and although it does take time and effort to make it some people do so on a commercial basis while others prefer to make it themselves.

Soak *12 lbs of stoned dates* in a large container with *just enough water to cover them,* for 36 hours. The softened dates should be broken up in a food processor in cupfuls at a time, and left to stand overnight.

Place the processed dates in a stout linen bag, a little at a time, and squeeze them dry. Alternatively a small manual press may be used - such as that used for home made wines. Even with the aid of a press it could take a few hours to complete this stage of preparation.

Use a large container or preserving pan to cook the juice, to which *a cup of co*
water should be added. Begin cooking over a high flame until it comes to the boil, an
then lower to moderate heat. From time to time it will be necessary to remove the fro
from the surface and stir the liquid. Keep the date juice on the boil for about five hou
or until the consistency is of a heavy syrup. At this stage the froth may become tinged wi
an orange hue.

Cool and leave to stand overnight and then decant into cold bottles. This quanti
should fill between 4 and $4\frac{1}{2}$ wine bottles.

Many people find it convenient to make Halek during Passover and generally kee
it in store for the following year(s). It has an indefinite shelf life if it is airtight and store
in a cool place. Sometimes the natural sugar content in the date juice becomes crystallise
in which case the bottle may be immersed in a bowl of hot, but not boiling, water unt
it is restored to its smooth consistency.

Ground walnuts or almonds are added to individual portions of the date syrup t
complete the "haroseth". This is usually eaten with "matza" or unleavened bread. Mat.
was made communally in Calcutta in the compound of the synagogues and sold t
individual families. The required quantity would be wrapped in large sheets and store
in enormous baskets as this was the entire bread supply of a family for eight days.

Shavuoth is the Festival of Pentecost and is celebrated for agricultural an
historical reasons. This was the time of the grain harvest - barley, corn and whea
according to the Book of Ruth. It was also the time when the children of Israel receive
the gift of the Torah or Law through Moses on Mount Sinai.

One of the ways in which Jews remember is through eating symbolic foods. Th
Book of Ruth 2.14 says "and she (Ruth) sat beside the reapers and they reached h
parched corn and she did eat and was satisfied, and left thereof". By doing as Ruth did w
commemorate the agricultural significance of the festival. I am told it was a custom fro
Baghdad to eat the meal from roasted corn. In our family we ate this meal, mixed wi
water and sugar and recited the blessing "Blessed are You, Lord our God, Creator of th
Universe who created everything according to His will".

The Song of Songs says 4.11 "honey and milk are under your tongue
Metaphorically, the Jewish people is likened to milk and the Torah likened to honey. Th
is symbolised by eating dairy products (from milk) and sweet products (from honey) a
in honour of Ruth and the harvest festival we include products made of grain.

It is therefore customary to eat KAHI, made of wheat flour which is sprinkled wi
sugar or eaten with jam and fried CHEESE SUMOOSUCKS made of wheat flour an
cheese.

AHI

Make the dough with *1 lb self raising flour, a pinch of salt, 3 oz butter* (clarified butter or ghee would be better) *2 teaspoons of vinegar and water to bind it.* Let the dough stand, covered, for about an hour.

Divide the dough into balls about the size of a table-tennis ball. Roll each one out s fine as possible. Then stretch the pastry from the middle, securing with one hand and stretching with the other.

Small tears can easily be secured together again. Stretch the pastry into as square shape as possible. Nine inches square should be the rough aim. Butter one third of the square and fold it towards the middle. Then butter the opposite outer third and fold into the middle. (You should now have an oblong shaped pastry). Butter one third and fold into the middle. Butter the other third and again fold into the middle until you have a square. Continue to make the kahi preparations in this way until all the dough has been used.

Fry the kahis in hot butter ; when it is in the pan, hold it down to stabilise with one hand and spoon over hot butter on the top to make the kahi puff up. Turn the kahi so that the top is now browned, lifting the top layer and spooning the hot butter into the middle to cook the pastry inside. The outside of the kahi should be crisp and golden brown while the inside should be soft and white. Drain the butter and serve hot with sugar or jam. Some families use date juice or Halek left over from Passover to eat with their Kahis during Shavuoth.

Daisy Iny also describes Kahis eaten in Baghdad on Shavuoth. The same name is used suggesting continuity. They used filo pastry which was baked but we made our own pastry in Calcutta, and since oven cooking was scarcely available we used frying as the more common method of preparation. For those who prefer oven cooking as I do, there is no reason why the traditional Baghdadi method should not be reinstated.

RIED CHEESE SUMOOSUCKS

The dough is prepared in exactly the same way as for Kahi.

For the cheese filling use any *white hard cheese,* grate it, then mix it with *a lightly beaten egg .* Add *salt and pepper* to taste (and *a dash of mustard* too , although this is not traditional). The consistency of the filling should be firm.

Divide the dough into small balls - about the size of a large marble. Roll out fine into a circle. Fill one side of the circle with the cheese and egg filling and fold the other side over. Crimp the edges.

Fry in hot butter, stabilising the pan with one hand and spooning the hot butter over the sumoosuck with the other, to make it puff up.

Serve hot.

LIST OF THE RECIPES

LIGHT MEALS continued

RICE DISHES

MAIN MEALS